# FINANCIAL HACKING

**Evaluate Risks, Price Derivatives, Structure Trades, and Build Your Intuition Quickly and Easily**

# FINANCIAL HACKING

**Evaluate Risks, Price Derivatives, Structure Trades, and Build Your Intuition Quickly and Easily**

### Philip Maymin
New York University, USA

NEW JERSEY · LONDON · SINGAPORE · BEIJING · SHANGHAI · HONG KONG · TAIPEI · CHENNAI

*Published by*

World Scientific Publishing Co. Pte. Ltd.
5 Toh Tuck Link, Singapore 596224
*USA office:* 27 Warren Street, Suite 401-402, Hackensack, NJ 07601
*UK office:* 57 Shelton Street, Covent Garden, London WC2H 9HE

**British Library Cataloguing-in-Publication Data**
A catalogue record for this book is available from the British Library.

**FINANCIAL HACKING**
**Evaluate Risks, Price Derivatives, Structure Trades, and Build Your Intuition Quickly and Easily**

Copyright © 2012 by World Scientific Publishing Co. Pte. Ltd.

*All rights reserved. This book, or parts thereof, may not be reproduced in any form or by any means, electronic or mechanical, including photocopying, recording or any information storage and retrieval system now known or to be invented, without written permission from the Publisher.*

For photocopying of material in this volume, please pay a copying fee through the Copyright Clearance Center, Inc., 222 Rosewood Drive, Danvers, MA 01923, USA. In this case permission to photocopy is not required from the publisher.

ISBN 978-981-4322-55-3

In-house Editor: Yvonne Tan

Printed by FuIsland Offset Printing (S) Pte Ltd Singapore

# Dedication and Acknowledgments

*For Yelena, Elena, Ellie, and Lena: my wife of many names.*

I am grateful to the excellent assistance of my TAs, Prathamesh Godbole, Ray (Dongrui) Huang (twice!), and Varun Batra, and to the students in my course for their help in spotting typos in earlier versions and particularly for their active and enthusiastic participation in class.

This book would not have been possible without my father Zak, with whom I have been evaluating trading strategies, managing risk, pricing derivatives, writing papers, and having fun for the past 3+ decades.

To my daughters who wondered why papa would often stay home and punch the computer while they went out to play: I'm back!

July 30, 2012<br>
Greenwich, Connecticut

# Foreword

This book is unlike any other textbook on financial engineering, primarily because this is not about financial engineering at all. It is about financial hacking.

> "A hacker is any person who derives joy from discovering ways to circumvent limitations."
>
> *Robert Bickford*

Financial engineering is a far fancier sounding term for what is in practice the same thing, but to those new to the field, it conveys a precision and automation that is simply absent in the real world.

Building appropriate risk tolerances and financial portfolios is not at all the same as building sturdy bridges or efficient transport. There is a lot more art and conceptual work in finance; on the trading floor, the right intuition is far more valuable than the right formula.

This book's goal is to build your intuition, and in doing so, to show you how you can quickly and easily address complicated issues in risk and finance. Although money has been around for eons, finance itself is a young field. Its future is and will continue to be brighter than its past for many decades yet. A stubborn adhesion to past models and assumptions will backfire. The best approach is a fluid and flexible one.

I want to teach you finance through apprenticeship rather than rote memorization. This book is your sandbox. Think of it as the meeting minutes from a weekly research and trading seminar held at a big Wall Street firm or a hedge fund. You can play and make mistakes here so that when it is time to perform for real, you have gotten all the mistakes out of the way, and done it so thoroughly, that you know how to avoid the common pitfalls even in models and derivatives that are brand new.

## How Not to Read This Book

Do not read this book in a quiet place while sitting alone and concentrating. Trading floors are busy, bustling places with constant interruptions.

> "And now, excuse me while I interrupt myself."
>
> *Murray Walker*

Read it on a subway, in a moving vehicle, at a deli, in a bar, on the dance floor, during your Oscar acceptance speech, while you are being knighted, etc.; basically, anytime you can be rudely interrupted. It's good training.

Occasional quotations like the above punctuate this book. They serve three purposes: first is to interrupt your thinking in case you ignored my advice above and actually found a quiet place to read; second is to give a little break in the action; and third is to sometimes provide an alternative hidden viewpoint.

## What You Won't Find in This Book

If you are looking for a little sleeve with a CD on it, you'll keep looking for a long time. If you are looking for a web address with all of the code from this book available there for easy download, you won't be able to find it. It's not available.

This lack of source code is a feature. How can a lack of something be a feature? And specifically, how can a book about projects not include a CD or a website with the code in it? That seems crazy. But it's the very point of the book that financial engineers learn by doing, not by copy-and-pasting.

The projects involve and discuss such tools and programming languages as Microsoft Excel, S-PLUS or R, and Mathematica. It is not the purpose of the book to teach any one language, but rather to show how to build projects in various standard tools of the trade and in expressive, easily understandable languages.

Indeed, it is not required or expected that readers know any of these languages or tools at all. The code snippets are intended to be essentially self-explanatory, though occasional tips and tricks do come in.

Examples and code snippets and projects permeate the book, and that means the book can be appreciated in two different ways. Think of it like a book on how to draw cartoons. You could just flip through the book, look at the pretty pictures, and come away with some tips you gleaned here or there. Or you can take the time to do the exercises along the way and truly master the craft.

The code I present in this book is not intended to be used by you directly. In fact, almost none of the code you will ever produce, and hopefully you will produce a lot, will be used, or should be used. Instead, the goal is that when you need to generate similar code, you will be able to do so quickly, without needing to look anything up.

Financial hacking is what traders and their assistants need to be able to do while the counterparty is still on the phone. It is about speed and intuition. You or someone else can later carefully move it to production-worthy code after several layers of quality assurance.

For a similar reason, you also won't find references or an index or a bibliography. It is the $21^{st}$ century! If you want more information about a particular topic or model or derivative, there are plenty of places to look on the web, places that change and evolve continuously.

## Puzzles

Here is something that you *will* find in this book that is so rare anywhere else: puzzles. Deep puzzles that go to the heart of finance.

Want an example?

An investor claims that markets are not normally distributed and indeed have much fatter tails than most people believe. His strategy, therefore, is to buy wings, meaning deep out-of-the-money options that act more like lottery tickets than investment vehicles. (We will of course learn the details about what an option is, and so on, throughout the book.)

He claims that this strategy tends to lose a little bit routinely, because most of the times, the lottery-like wings do not pay off. So maybe he loses say $1 million a year during a quiet year. But once in a while crazy things happen and he makes $20 million.

Do you believe him?

(a) Sure, sounds reasonable.
(b) No, he is lying, it is absolutely impossible.

If you answered (a) or (b), then you are wrong.

First, to the cynics who think the investor is lying. It is *not* impossible. Even on liquid equity indices, if you look at monthly returns, large events can happen. If you bet that the market will move by more than ten percent in either direction by the end of the next month, you will usually end up with nothing, but once in a while, when the market moves a lot, you can make a lot of money.

Now, to the believers who think his strategy sounds reasonable. It doesn't, and here's why.

While it is true that over the course of say a month, a large enough move could happen that would generate $20 million in profit, that move is almost surely the result of a continuous trend. In other words, there exists a day when the profit on the position was only $10 million, or $5 million, or even $2 million, a time when the investor had the opportunity to get out with a profit.

To believe his strategy, you have to think he is a hypocrite. He claims to only hold wings. But once a wing position starts to become profitable, to be consistent, he ought to sell those winning wings, and buy new wings. But if he does that, then he is very unlikely to make $20 million profits. A lot of that profit comes from the continuing profits of wings that first became profitable and then continued on.

Thus, either the investor is letting past winning wings ride, contrary to his professed strategy, or he is not making as much money as he claims.

Is the above argument correct? It seems plausible. But it's not enough to just argue verbally. By the time you finish this book, you should be able to figure out how to test it through appropriate simulations. I will not tell you or show you how that comes out. I won't even mention this little puzzle again. It's a little test for yourself to see if you would be able to do it.

That's what building your intuition is all about.

## Who You Are

This book is intended for graduate (including both MBA and MS) or motivated undergraduate students in finance, mathematical finance, or financial engineering, and also for new practitioners in the field, or those moving from other areas into quantitative research in financial firms.

There are three ways of teaching and learning finance. MBAs in finance learn case-method and standard finance, mainly by talking. Mathematical finance students learn the elegance and beauty of formulas, mainly by manipulating symbols. But financial engineers need to learn how to build useful tools, and the best way to do that is to actually build them in a test environment, with no real profits at stake.

In the current economic environment, despite slowdowns and job losses by many of the MBAs and mathematical finance people, there has never been a greater need for financial engineers, people who know both the standard finance of the MBAs and the quantitative methods of the mathematical programs, and who can integrate them with an intuition about the market, a focused creativity, and, above all, the ability to get things done.

## Why Should You Read This?

This book teaches financial engineering in an innovative way: by providing tools and a point of view to quickly and easily solve real front-office problems. Projects and simulations are not just exercises in this book, but its heart and soul. You as the reader, whether a current or a budding student or practitioner, will not only gain the intuition and expertise to be able to answer general complex questions about risk and finance, you will also learn how to make reasonable inferences based on incomplete information, thus making you extraordinarily valuable to banks, brokerage houses, trading floors, and hedge funds.

## Let Me Tell You a Little about Myself

I graduated Harvard University with both a Bachelor's in Computer Science and a Master's in Applied Math in a combined three and a half years. I went to work right away at Long-Term Capital Management, where I traded various equity derivatives strategies in the U.S., Asia, and Europe. Even during the 1998 collapse, my books, and indeed most of the books in the Tokyo office where I was stationed, were profitable. I then joined Ellington Management Group along with my father where we launched and ran their equity derivatives and statistical arbitrage desks, trading convertible bonds, options, and exotic derivatives. We later started and ran our own hedge fund, Maymin Capital Management.

Since closing that fund, I earned my Ph.D. in Finance from the University of Chicago Booth School of Business and am now an Assistant Professor of Finance and Risk Engineering at NYU-Polytechnic Institute. I have about a dozen academic publications and am the founding managing editor of *Algorithmic Finance*, a new journal focusing on the bridge between computer science and finance.

I have also been a policy scholar for a free market think tank, a Justice of the Peace, a Congressional candidate, and a columnist for *American Banker*, the *Fairfield County Weekly*, and LewRockwell.com. I am also an award-winning journalist and the author of *Yankee Wake Up*, *Free Your Inner Yankee*, and *Yankee Go Home*. I was a finalist for the 2010 Bastiat Prize for Online Journalism. I also have a J.D. and am an attorney-at-law admitted to practice in California.

My popular writings have been published in dozens of media outlets ranging from *Bloomberg* to *Forbes* to the *New York Post* to *American Banker* to regional newspapers, and my research has been profiled in dozens more, including *The New York Times*, *USA Today*, *Financial Times*, *Boston Globe*, *NPR*, *BBC*, *Guardian* (UK), *CNBC*, *Newsweek Poland*, *Financial Times Deutschland*, and others.

> "I am so smart! S-M-R-T... I mean S-M-A-R-T!"
> 
> *Homer Simpson*, "The Simpsons" (1993)

Enough with the introductions. Let's get going!

# Contents

| | |
|---|---|
| *Foreword* | vii |
| **PART 1: Vanilla World** | **1** |
| **Chapter 1:** Risk | 3 |
| **Chapter 2:** Arbitrage | 19 |
| **Chapter 3:** Trading Puzzles | 27 |
| | |
| **PART 2: Vanilla Derivatives** | **41** |
| **Chapter 4:** Black-Scholes | 43 |
| **Chapter 5:** Simulation | 65 |
| **Chapter 6:** Puzzles and Bugs | 89 |
| | |
| **PART 3: Exotic Derivatives** | **121** |
| **Chapter 7:** Single-Asset Exotic Options | 123 |
| **Chapter 8:** Multi-Asset Exotic Options | 139 |
| | |
| **PART 4: Exotic Worlds** | **149** |
| **Chapter 9:** The Best Trade in the World? | 151 |
| **Chapter 10:** Variance Swaps | 163 |
| **Chapter 11:** Esoteric Worlds and Derivatives | 177 |

# Part 1

# Vanilla World

# Chapter 1

# Risk

Risk is the "why?" behind finance. Without risk, there is no reason for finance or insurance or derivatives to exist at all. Of course there is risk in the real world. But it can be hard to understand when wrapped in all the complexities of reality. We can gain a lot of intuition about it by exploring it in the context of a plain vanilla world.

## 1.1 What is Risk?

There is no single perfect definition of risk. But you think you have one. If you have studied some finance or risk management before, you may think that risk is the probability and impact of a loss. That's a reasonable sounding definition, right? I've used it myself many times. But it's wrong. Let's see why.

Suppose you are my broker and I wish to invest my life earnings of $100 in IBM. I ask you a simple question: "What is my risk?"

What is the risk of putting $100 in IBM?

To go with the standard definition above, you might say that you need to calculate the answer based on a complicated formula involving the historical returns of IBM and perhaps even other securities, forecasts about the future, information about my preferences and income streams, and so forth. Suppose for specificity that after all your calculations the numbers that come out are like this: I would have a 20 percent chance of losing $30. Is that my risk?

If that's really my full risk, you should be willing to stand behind your claim. You should be willing to make me whole on losses beyond $30, or you should at least be willing to give me 4:1 odds that I won't experience a loss at all. Not quite ready to do that? Then maybe you haven't fully defined risk.

"Alright," you say, "I get it. You're just trying to separate quantifiable risk from raw uncertainty, like the difference between tossing a coin and predicting the stock market."

Am I?

True, there is a difference between the two concepts, but that distinction is more a pedagogical or a philosophical one. As traders and as financial hackers, we are just as comfortable assigning probabilities to uncertain outcomes as we are taking objective probabilities as given. After all, in the nitty-gritty world of actual life, there are no infinite samples or true probabilities, only a measure of how much we are willing to gamble and at what odds.

Instead, what I am arguing is that risk itself is hard to define.

Nevertheless, you may be asked at an interview to define risk. This is a weak, early-round question usually asked by younger interviewers who don't really know how to best conduct an interview. They are only looking for one answer: "Risk is uncertainty about the future."

This is a silly answer. For one thing, if your electricity fails, and you do not see market data, then you also have exposure to market movements occurring in the past, not just the future. Just because you don't know what has already happened doesn't make it riskless.

> Minsky then shut his eyes.
> "Why do you close your eyes?" Sussman asked his teacher.
> "So that the room will be empty."
> At that moment, Sussman was enlightened.
>
> *The ending to a famous hacker koan*

I don't think there is a good definition of risk. Some people see less risk in skydiving than others. Some people can hedge risks that others cannot. Ultimately risk is just the set of your unhedged exposures, including ones you don't know about.

How should you respond when you are asked this question? It depends; if you are asked in a social setting, or after you already have the job, go ahead and opine freely. But if you are asked at an interview, start first with what they want to hear; then you can discuss the more intricate details.

This holds as a life lesson too: when people ask you questions expecting to hear a particular answer, they won't listen to what you are saying until you first speak the magic words their brains are tuned in to. Can you imagine being asked, "Does this make me look fat?" and responding with a treatise on nutrition and fashion and lighting and culture? The person asking will be fidgeting nervously, not processing a word you say, growing increasingly angry and hurt, until you at last mercifully let out a sharp and firm "No!" And then they'll ask you why it took so long.

Historically, risk was more of a nautical term referring to uncharted waters. When you discover new lands and new civilizations, when you boldly go where no one has gone before, you may die, or you may find riches. Today, risk only refers to bad outcomes. There is no "risk" to winning the lottery, but there is a very high risk of losing. This is merely a semantic difference and should not bother you too much. After all, in the financial world, someone's downside risk is someone else's upside potential.

So risk may not have a perfect definition. Does that mean finance is doomed? A sham? A false pursuit?

Not at all.

So what if risk isn't easily defined? Many fields cannot define the basics of what they study.

Biology is the study of life; life does not have a perfect definition. Physics is the study of matter; matter does not have a perfect definition.

## 1.2 What is Finance?

Finance is the study of risk, even though risk does not have a perfect definition.

You may have thought finance was also the study of money and savings and budgets and loans. There is some of that, but risk is central.

The origin of the word apparently traces back to the word "fine," which related to the completion of a debt or the fulfilling of an obligation. It has the same meaning as one of the oldest words for freedom, the Sumerian "amargi," which was literally an order to release to their mothers the children that had been held as slaves and collateral on the debt. Finance is thus a very libertarian concept.

How is it pronounced? Is it fin-ANCE or FINE-ance?

(a) It is pronounced FINE-ance when it is a verb, as in, "I want to finance this vehicle," but fin-ANCE when it is a noun, as in, "I work in finance."
(b) The exact opposite is true.
(c) Neither of the above is true.

The answer seems to be (a) in the U.S.A. and (b) in the U.K., so globally the answer must be (c). I don't think anybody knows. Pronounce it however you like, in any context.

If you ask people what finance means today, the answer will be some variation of "money." It could be personal finance dealing with personal money, corporate finance dealing with corporate money, and so on. Yet we don't call what financial hackers do monetary engineering, but rather financial engineering. So there is some difference between money and finance.

Indeed, one view of finance is that it is about the slicing and dicing of money, and, of course, risk. Through securities, derivatives, and contracts, finance reallocates risk in exchange for money.

## 1.3  Value-at-Risk Puzzles

Philosophy aside, we need to manage risk in the real world. If we don't do it, someone else will, and they may not do as good a job.

The most common systematic approach to evaluating the risk of an arbitrary portfolio or position is to ask what is its *value-at-risk* or VaR. Note that the middle letter is lowercase to help distinguish it from VAR or Var, which may refer to variance.

The idea behind the VaR is reasonable enough. It asks what is the worst case loss that can result from the given position, assuming we would be unable to liquidate it for a given period of time.

Actually, what it asks is slightly different. It asks what is the *almost* worst case loss. If it were asking about the true worst case loss, for a long-only unleveraged portfolio, that answer would be 100 percent, regardless of the time period. That's not a very useful answer for the real world, even though it is technically correct, because it doesn't help compare and contrast across different possibilities.

Instead, VaR asks, ignoring the really bad outcomes, let's say the worst 1 percent, other than those, what is the most we can expect to lose over a given period of time?

Your first day on the job as a risk manager, or perhaps even during an interview, you may be asked to calculate the VaR. "Hey new kid, get me the VaR on IBM," the boss might bark and start to walk away.

Before he is out of earshot, you need to ask him three questions, and possibly four.

First, what is the underlying? "IBM," he says, looking at you like you are hard of hearing. Okay, if he has already told you, don't ask again.

Second, what is the percentage for the VaR? This is usually a number like 95 or 99 percent, and it represents the portion of the distribution you *do not* throw away. So a 95 percent VaR means, what is the worst case loss, except for the really worst case 5 percent? "99 percent," he says.

Third, what is the holding period? This means how long you are expected to have to withstand the risk to the position. If you only have to hold the position one day against your will, that will have less VaR than if you have to hold a month. "10 days," he says. That's the usual answer and it represents ten business days, or two weeks.

The possible fourth question is how far back to look in historical data. You could make this judgment call yourself, but it is an important consideration. The further back you look, the more data you'll have, but the distribution of IBM returns 50 years ago is probably not very relevant to their distribution tomorrow.

To give him some comfort that you know what you are doing, you can combine all these questions with the typical default assumptions into one quick shout: "99 percent, 10-day VaR on IBM, looking back five years?"

"Sure," he says, and nods approvingly, and disappears.

> "And poof. Just like that, he's gone."
> *Verbal Kint* (Kevin Spacey), "The Usual Suspects"

The best way to compute the VaR is if you have a distribution for the future that you believe. But you usually don't have that, so you use past data as an indication of what the future might look like. You don't believe the past will repeat verbatim, in the same order, but perhaps the distribution is the same, or at least similar enough.

> "History doesn't repeat itself — at best it sometimes rhymes."
> *Mark Twain*

There are two primary ways to compute the VaR: parametric and non-parametric. Non-parametric is easier to understand. Take your historical data. Divide it into returns of the same length as your target time period. For example, slice it up into overlapping ten-day returns. Now you have a list of ten-day returns that happened in the past. Order those from most negative to most positive. Throw away the first 1 percent, if you are doing 99 percent VaR. The remaining number is your VaR. It means, if the future rhymes with the past, the worst case ten-day loss that can happen, ignoring the really worst 1 percent, is this number.

Now, with non-parametric, you sometimes have jumps between the returns. Your ninth-worst return and your tenth-worst return might be separated by a few percent. If you want a more continuous number that doesn't jump so much, you can interpolate between the two closest numbers. It doesn't matter for conceptual purposes.

Parametric is simpler to calculate but requires more assumptions. For parametric VaR, you have to assume what the future distribution will look like, and then calibrate the particular parameters based on the historical data.

Almost always, the parametric family is the normal distribution. So you would just calculate the historical average and standard deviation of returns and assume your future distribution will be the normal with those parameters. Then your 99 percent VaR is just 2.33 standard deviations below the mean, and your 95 percent VaR is 1.96 standard deviations below the mean.

Whether you do parametric or non-parametric, you should end up with a negative number, representing, as it does, a loss. When we speak the VaR, however, we omit the negative sign. So we might say the 99 percent 10-day VaR on a $100 million investment in IBM is $10 million, meaning that the most we will lose over a ten-day period, except for one percent of the time, is $10 million.

The parametric approach is by far the most common approach in the real world. In addition to its simplicity, it also lets you calculate the VaR's of arbitrary portfolios instantaneously if you know the correlations between all of its components. With a non-parametric approach, to calculate the VaR of a portfolio equally weighted in Google and IBM, you would have to create a historical time series of that portfolio. With a parametric approach, you just combine their individual VaR's with each other, taking into account the correlation.

Now, here is a quick quiz to see if you truly understood all that.

During an interview, your potential boss says, "I just heard from our auditors that the 99% ten-day VaR of our portfolio is huge — it is now one trillion dollars." He then asks you to explain in plain terms what that means. You say:

(a) "It means that over the next two weeks, there is only a small chance that you would lose more than a trillion dollars."
(b) "It means that for an average ten-day movement in your portfolio, you are very likely to need a new loan of one trillion dollars to survive."
(c) "It means that based on your models, an average ten-day movement in your portfolio is 99 percent certain to result in a loss, with a worst case of one trillion dollars."
(d) "It means that based on your models, an average ten-day movement in your portfolio is 1 percent certain to result in a loss, with a worst case of one trillion dollars."

The answer is (a). We know (c) and (d) must be wrong because VaR never reports the true worst case loss; it only states the worst case but for a little bit. And (b) must be wrong because the boss is very *unlikely* to lose the entire trillion.

What confuses people on answer (a) is that it reflects the next two weeks rather than some Platonic ideal of an average two weeks. VaR is never about forecasting some ideal average. It is literally about forecasting the immediate future. Tomorrow, you will have a new VaR estimate for tomorrow's immediate future.

Here are two puzzles. First, an easy one.

You are a risk manager and I am a trader. I need your approval for my trade. For every trade I propose, you give me a number indicating the amount of capital that I have to keep in reserve to maintain that position.

If the number you give is too high, I won't do the trade, and the firm loses the potential profits, loses market share to its competitors, and is eventually bought out by a competitor, at which point you are found to be redundant and so you get laid off.

If the number you give is too low, I will do too much of the trade, putting on positions that are too risky. At first things may go well, and I will earn a fat bonus check, but eventually, risk will rear its ugly head, I will lose more money than I have set aside, other parts of the company will have to liquidate their assets to compensate, we will go bankrupt, get bailed out, repeat the process, go through many lawsuits, and ultimately find ourselves without a job, holding a worthless stock portfolio in the company's shares. Fire and brimstone stuff.

So you have to get the number right.

You don't want the responsibility of evaluating every trade on its own merits, if for no other reason than because you participate in none of the upside. You want to establish an algorithm, a procedure that takes trades or proposed portfolios as inputs and spits out a reasonable number. Almost always, you will do something like a VaR. You may also have stress test and scenario analyses to buttress your VaR number.

Suppose I come to you and present an asset whose historical distributions of returns usually had no skewness (a measure of the symmetry of the returns) or excess kurtosis (a measure of the fat tails). But recently the asset randomly experienced a very high average return and a very negative skewness. Then which of the following would be the best way to measure 99 percent VaR?

(a) 2.33 times the historical volatility.
(b) Parametric 99% VaR assuming normal distribution using estimates of the first two moments.
(c) Non-parametric 99% VaR.

I can sense the urge you feel towards saying (c). You want to say non-parametric, you need to say non-parametric. You think non-parametric is clearly a superior algorithm; after all, we know the problem with parametric VaR is that the fat tails we observe in reality are understated.

But in this case, non-parametric is flat-out wrong. Why? Because it would incorporate the very high return that the asset has historically experienced, and we do not believe that that return will persist into the future; we do not believe it because the question stated that the high return occurred randomly.

Fine, you sigh, and reluctantly agree that the answer must be (b), if for no other reason than it is the longest, and the longest answers are often the right ones.

Not this time.

If you use a parametric normal distribution fitting the first two moments, then you are again incorporating the random, wrong historical average return. You may well end up with a negative risk number, suggesting that 99 percent of the time you will make money. That's just silly.

The answer is (a). This is the answer that calculates a parametric VaR using the normal distribution but assuming a zero mean return and a volatility calibrated from the historical return distribution. The volatility we do expect to be approximately the same as it has been.

Now for the harder puzzle.

---

"Who in the world am I? Ah, that's the great puzzle."

*Lewis Carroll*

For your VaR algorithm, suppose you do either parametric or non-parametric. It is your choice, and it doesn't matter for this puzzle. I come to you with a single stock that I claim is going to be a wonderful investment based on its fundamentals. Historically it has grown at 3 percent per month and has had a standard deviation of 1 percent per month. Whether you do parametric or non-parametric, you will find that my risk going forward appears to be negative!

So what should you do?

(a) You should believe in the model and pay me to put on this seemingly negative risk trade.
(b) You should negotiate a little and at least see if I would be willing to put on such a trade with zero haircut, meaning I put up zero reserve capital, but I also receive zero from you.
(c) You should just nix the trade based on your gut that something smells fishy here.

All of those answers are wrong. You can't just nix the trade without a reason; it is not your job as a risk manager to introduce yet another layer of subjective bias. On the contrary, the firm looks to you for objective guidance and support.

Of course you don't want to pay me to put on this trade. Otherwise I will just put this trade on as much as possible, take your money, and go home. And I would do the same thing if you just let me put it on with zero capital because compared with other possible trades, I am getting more risk exposure for less reserve capital. Since as a trader I essentially reap the upside more than I pay for the downside, this is an easy decision for me.

Perhaps the best answer would be to draw on the wisdom from the previous puzzle and change your VaR methodology to simply ignore all past average returns and instead assume that going forward all expected returns are zero, or the riskless rate, or some other reasonable default value.

If not, if you instead try to tweak the algorithm perhaps to squeeze past returns to zero, or institute minimum and maximum thresholds, then you are simply creating a new game for me to play. As a trader, I like games, and I will play yours and not only will I win, I will crush you.

How would I do it? I'd just look through thousands of assets until I found one that looks better under your requirements than under my own more reasonable judgment. Do you think it is difficult for me to find a stock that has had a very high average return over the past few years? It's not. I'll just sort them all, maybe take the second best one to throw off suspicion, weave you a tale of excellent fundamentals and growth potential, and end up with an over-sized and under-risked investment.

Incidentally, if you were thinking that this might be part of the problem that caused the recent financial turmoil, you'd be right. Having an objective set of regulations means the regulator can, and will, be gamed. Indeed it can be shown that *any* regulation of risk will always result in greater systemic risk.

## 1.4 Derivatives

A derivative is a security whose value is derived from other securities. Is a mutual fund that invests in hundreds of other stocks a derivative?

(a) Yes, because its value is derived from the other stocks.
(b) No, because it is not itself a security.
(c) Yes, if it is a closed-end mutual fund.

The best answer is (c). Certainly a mere portfolio of assets is not a derivative, even though its value is clearly derived from those assets. A financial derivative needs to be something you can trade by itself. If the portfolio were offered to you in the form of a swap (a swap is just a financial contract between two parties) then that swap would be a derivative, because the value of the swap ultimately derives from the value of the component assets. But the portfolio itself is not a derivative.

Maybe the best illustration is to think of a Happy Meal at McDonald's. If you just lay out a burger, small fries, and kids drink on a table, that is a portfolio. To get it, you have to make several orders. But if you put it all in a box with a toy, suddenly, it is something you can order immediately. It is more than just a portfolio; it has become a derivative.

> "I got to thinking. Kids want something to do while they're eating."
>
> *Bob Bernstein*, inventor of the Happy Meal

The reason that (c) is a better answer than (b) is because some mutual funds actually are securities. There are two types of mutual funds: closed-end and open-end. Open-end mutual funds are the standard you are probably familiar with: you can put in money and the manager invests it, and you can take your money out and the manager will sell your portion of the underlying portfolio.

But with a closed-end mutual fund, the only way to get your money out is to sell your holding to someone else. And the only way to put your money in is to buy someone else's holding. In other words, there is a separate security associated with closed-end mutual funds, and when you buy or sell it, the manager of the fund does not change his allocation to the portfolio at all, neither increasing nor decreasing in size. You just move claims to that portfolio around. Thus a closed-end mutual fund is more like a Happy Meal. It comes in its own separate box.

## 1.5 Forwards and Futures

The first true derivative most people are exposed to are forwards and futures. A forward contract is an agreement between a buyer and a seller to exchange money for assets at some future point in time. A futures contract is an exchange-traded version of a forward, where one of the parties to the agreement is the exchange.

Forwards can have arbitrary *leverage*. If you are British or just visiting the Queen, you would use the word *gearing* instead of leverage. Why you are discussing this concept with the monarchy, though, is beyond the scope of this book.

Leverage is the ratio of the amount of notional risk you control to the amount of actual assets you have on the line, minus one. If you take $100 and buy $100 worth of IBM, then your leverage is zero. You are unleveraged. You can also say you are unlevered. This is not to be confused with the half British-half Dutch consumer goods conglomerate Unilever.

If you take $50 of your own money, and borrow another $50, and buy $100 worth of IBM, then your leverage is one. This is also referred to as 1:1, pronounced "one-to-one." This means for every $1 you put up, you also get an additional $1 of borrowed money.

If you were to take $25 of your own money and borrow $75 to buy $100 worth of IBM, then your leverage is three, or 3:1. Sometimes, people refer to leverage as a multiple. In that case, you might say you are leveraged "four times" to mean that you have four times the position size that you would have if you were to only invest unlevered.

It can be a confusing nomenclature. Be careful. Don't just blurt out ambiguous phrases like, "Do we have unit leverage or are we unlevered on Unilever?" Instead, always find out how much notional can be supported by a single dollar of investment.

Personally, I prefer the term *haircut*, or margin. This refers to the portion of the notional that needs to be supported by your own capital. So if you have $100 worth of IBM supported by $16 of your own money, with the rest borrowed, then you have a 16 percent haircut.

The advantages of haircut over gearing or leverage are that it can easily and clearly express any arbitrary number without requiring an integer amount, it cannot be misinterpreted, and it leaves less room for tongue twisters or unintentional confusion, even if you are investing in one of Unilever's many fine shampoo or hair products.

A forward can have any strike price, but there will always be one unique strike price that results in the forward contract itself having a zero current value. This unique strike price is called the fair forward price.

It is pretty easy to figure out what the fair forward price is. Just figure out your second-best alternative. You could either buy a forward struck at $F$ or borrow $S$ to buy the stock.

If you borrow, you have to pay back $S$ plus the interest rate at the maturity, but you would also have received all of the dividends on the stock in the meantime.

In other words, you could exchange either $F$ for a share of stock at maturity, or $S$ plus the interest owed minus the dividends earned until maturity. Therefore $F$ equals $S$ plus the interest owed minus the dividends earned until maturity.

Usually, dividends are not very high, so the fair forward strike tends to be larger than the current spot price.

This approach is the easiest way to remember how to price forwards. You don't have to memorize any formulas. Just recall the logic of comparing your alternatives.

What is the fair price that you as a seller would need to be paid today for you to agree to short a one-year forward struck at $50 on an underlying non-dividend-paying security currently trading at $100, if the interest rate is some positive constant number?

(a) Zero.
(b) Fifty.
(c) More than fifty.
(d) Less than fifty.

Let's figure out quickly, in a financial hacking kind of way, without trying to recall or rejigger any formulas. Instead, we will use, and build, our intuition.

If you require $X today to short a forward struck at $50, then in a year you will receive $50 and hand over unit of the security and be left with $X plus the interest you'd earned on it, plus $50.

To hedge yourself in the meantime against movements in the underlying, you would have to borrow $100 and buy the security today. In a year, you'd have to pay back $100 plus interest. Let's say interest on $1 for one year is just $r.

Then in a year, you would have no further position in the security, and you'd have $50 + X(1+r) - 100(1+r)$. For $X$ to be a fair price for the forward contract, that whole payoff should be worth zero. So we must have that:

$$X = 100 - 50/(1+r)$$

and since the interest rate is a positive constant, we are subtracting less than 50 from 100, and so $X$ must be greater than fifty. The answer is (c).

## 1.6 Forward Puzzle

If you call your broker right now and buy 100 shares of IBM, you wouldn't actually get those shares right away. Despite such humanity-shifting inventions such as the internet, email, smartphones, heck, even faxes, the clearing and settlement of stock trades in the United States still takes three business days.

If you call your broker on a Monday, and your order is filled that day, you won't actually get your shares in your account until Thursday.

That's not a spot transaction with immediate settlement. That's the very definition of a forward. Sure, it is only three days instead of a month or a year, but shouldn't the prices be adjusted based on our reasoning in the previous subsection to reflect forward prices?

We see prices trail across the bottom of our TVs in anachronistic tickers. We put in a buy order at $100 and get filled at $100. We don't have the actual shares yet. All we did was agree to accept the shares in exchange for $100 in three days.

Why don't we adjust the price to reflect forward pricing?

Maybe this is because of market convention, you say. Traders have implicitly agreed to it because half the time they are buyers and half the time sellers, so whatever differences there are tend to wash out in the end.

But I haven't agreed to any such thing. If I can buy a stock at a discounted price, then I would do so. Besides, even other traders, who care about every little transaction cost, slippage, and commission, wouldn't just take this extra random pricing discrepancy without a fight.

Maybe it is because it is only three days, you say, and so the difference is de minimus. I agree with you that on some days it may be small, particularly as overnight interest rates approach zero, but the difference is not exactly zero, and it is occasionally large.

Maybe everybody is just making a mistake, you suggest. Not everybody is as familiar with derivatives and risk as you now are. But if that were the case, there would still be arbitrageurs who would take advantage of those who are making a mistake. Besides, these are some of the most liquidly traded assets in the world. If there was a problem, we should have heard about it.

Give up?

The answer to the problem is that there is no problem. Why don't we use forward prices instead of spot prices? We do use forward prices!

Every single one of those ticks that float by on the TV or appear on the screen or in the pages of newspapers are forward prices. They are already adjusted for three days of interest and dividends, in exactly the fashion we described.

Want proof? Consider dividends. There are four dividend dates that matter for stocks.

First is the announcement date. That's when the company makes the big news that all is well and they are pleased to inform their shareholders that a dividend is eventually forthcoming. This could be a year before the actual dividend is paid.

Second is the ex date. Skip it for now; it's easier to explain later.

Third is the record date. That's when the company treasurer opens up the books and looks at who exactly are the shareholders of record and sends them each a check to their address.

Fourth is the pay date. That's when the checks actually go out. This can be a month or two after the record date. Even if there are new owners, the checks will still go out to those shareholders who were on the rolls as of the record date.

So now let's go back. What's the ex date? That's the date when the share stops trading with the dividends attached. Before the ex date, if you were to buy a share of the stock, you would be entitled to receive the upcoming dividend. After the ex date, you are no longer so entitled.

And when does the ex date occur? Exactly three business days before the record date. If Tuesday is the ex date, and Friday is the record date, then if you buy a share on Monday, you will still be a holder as of Friday (Thursday, even), and so you will eventually get the dividend.

But if you buy it on Tuesday, then you will be too late. You will not receive the dividend.

That is exactly what should happen with forwards, and it is exactly what happens in the stock market. All of those blinking lights and obsessive analysis on TV and radio over every little tick — not a single one of those prices are real spot prices.

They are all forward prices.

# Chapter 2

# Arbitrage

Arbitrage is defined in academia as "riskless profit" but it is used in practice to mean "good deal that should make money if all goes well." It is the basis for both pricing and hedging. But all is not as pure as it seems. There are a lot of philosophical issues behind this most central aspect of finance, and the basis for a financial golden rule.

## 2.1 An Example

The standard example of arbitrage is two identical securities trading at different prices. You buy the cheap one and then resell it at the expensive price. Boom! Easy money. If you can execute and settle both trades instantaneously, then that is pure arbitrage, and you should do it even if the difference is only for a penny.

Unfortunately even the slightest amount of "hair" or dirty real world problems will mess it up. Suppose it takes three days to settle each transaction. Then you have to wait three days until you can sleep peacefully. What is the cost of three days of mild nervousness? It's more than a penny.

And what about the capital you have committed to both sides of the trade? If it is more than zero, then you may be missing out on other opportunities. But this is not real hair: this is just the cost of capital. The real hair is in the possibilities that one of your counterparties fails, or the laws or regulations change, or something unforeseen happens to wreck the deal. You're not safe until you have the profit as cash in hand.

## 2.2 Is Arbitrage Impossible?

The answer to this question drastically affects public policy recommendations, financial regulations, employment opportunities, and, most of all, your own world view and overall level of happiness.

Almost all theorists argue that it is patently true that arbitrage is impossible. From their point of view, it would have to be. The impossibility of arbitrage is what academic economics and finance professors teach before all else. It is the basis of virtually every financial theory. Being theorists, they don't just declare it or observe it, they also prove it.

> "In theory, there is no difference between theory and practice. But, in practice, there is."
>
> *Jan L. A. van de Snepscheut* (attributed)
>
> *Yogi Berra* (attributed)
>
> *Chuck Reid* (attributed)

And here's how. Arbitrage to them is riskless profit — for example, when two identical things cost different amounts, the arbitrage is to buy the cheap one and sell it to whoever is overpaying for the other one. But if that were possible, continue the theorists, then someone else would have done it already. As more arbitrageurs do so, their trading increases the price of the cheap one and decreases the price of the expensive one. So arbitrageurs would bring mistaken prices back in line, and so there is no arbitrage opportunity to begin with; arbitrage is impossible because arbitrageurs would get rid of it immediately. In other words, if you think you see cash on the ground, don't bother picking it up, because if it was really there, someone else would have picked it up by now.

> "Even for practical purposes theory generally turns out the most important thing in the end."
>
> *Oliver Wendell Holms*

That sounds like a plausible argument. But unfortunately, it's just as easy to argue the opposite. Here is how: arbitrage is not only possible, it is commonplace. The proof? Well, we do occasionally find cash on the ground! We pick it up, and we are richer for it.

Arbitrage is all around us. Hedge funds and other wealth managers now totaling in the several trillion dollars of assets set up shop precisely to try to exploit mispricing between nearly identical assets. Even more standard money managers such as mutual funds or investment advisers try to allocate money in a way that they think will generate more profit at less risk. Every time you are offered a job for which there exist other equally good candidates, every time you choose to eat healthier and exercise more, every time you discover a shorter route home — that is arbitrage, and you are the arbitrageur.

If it weren't for arbitrage, if we honestly believed there is no way to make your life better, what would be the point of living? That is not to say that we always know what to do or how to do it; even in the financial world, traders have to discover the arbitrage opportunity before they can exploit it. But the search itself is only justified by at least the possibility of success.

> "Man — a being in search of meaning."
>
> *Plato*

Both the theorists and the realists seem to make good points, don't they? And it is easy to understand why people believe what they do. Academics believe arbitrage is essentially impossible because that belief allows them to do their work, creating tractable models which they can solve for the behavior of prices, because they know everything is priced correctly. Practitioners believe arbitrage is commonplace because that belief allows them to do their work, finding and exploiting mispricings in the market, because they know that occasionally things are priced incorrectly.

But the existence of arbitrage is not a religious question. Religious questions usually don't matter and so we are happy to tolerate irrelevant opinions. If you want to be a Pastafarian, it's your choice, and it doesn't affect atheists, Lutherans, or Buddhists.

But the question of arbitrage matters.

> "He hoped and prayed that there wasn't an afterlife. Then he realized there was a contradiction involved here and merely hoped that there wasn't an afterlife."
>
> *Douglas Adams*

If arbitrage is literally impossible, as the academics would have you believe, then those same academics would suggest we need more regulation of financial entities that claim or attempt to actually do arbitrage, since, from the academic perspective, such entities must be frauds.

But if arbitrage is possible, and indeed prevalent as the practitioners would have you believe, then those same practitioners would lobby for specific regulation protecting their particular way of trading, arguing that we need these rules to support the industry and protect investors from those who do not follow similar best practices. In other words, academics argue for restrictive regulation and practitioners argue for anti-competitive regulation.

This is more like a hostile religious question where one of two neighboring religions deny the legitimacy of the other one and will not rest until it is wiped out. On such religious questions, tolerance is futile and counterproductive. If you don't object to the Crusades, you end up Christian or dead.

> "One man's theology is another man's belly laugh."
>
> *Robert A. Heinlein*

On a less morbid note, if we don't object to the theorists, we end up with less freedom; ironically, if we don't object to the practitioners, we end up with less freedom too, since they only want freedom for themselves, not for everybody.

We are choosing the lesser of two evils. We have to decide: is arbitrage prevalent or impossible?

Quantum physicist and Nobel laureate Niels Bohr once said, essentially, that the opposite of a true statement is obviously false, but the opposite of a profound truth is another profound truth.

The existence of arbitrage opportunities is a profound truth.

Arbitrage is simultaneously both impossible and prevalent. Bohr argued that only in allowing and confronting the paradox head-on can we grow in our understanding.

> "How wonderful that we have met with a paradox. Now we have some hope of making progress."
>
> *Niels Bohr*

How can arbitrage be both impossible and prevalent? We have met with a paradox, but where is our progress?

There is an answer. The answer is frictions.

We all have friends and family members who are slowly but surely ruining their lives, at least from our perspective, but there is nothing we can do. Your brother takes the wrong job. Your friend marries the wrong spouse. Your cousin is an alcoholic. Your neighbor overeats. How are you going to "arbitrage" them?

You can't buy or borrow people. If you could, you would buy your neighbor, put him on a healthy diet and exercise regimen, and in a few months, return him in better shape, and pocket the difference in profit. You would have made a better man of him. But who are you going to buy him from? Who would you sell him to after? Alternatively, why not borrow him from himself, then fatten him up, make him cheaper, and return him, again pocketing the difference? These are the two things you could do with stocks, but not with people.

It's because of frictions. You can't change other people, not easily, and you can't profit from improving them.

> "The gem cannot be polished without friction, nor man perfected without trials."
>
> *Confucius*

In the financial world, you may have a colleague who could replace his concentrated holdings in company stock with a diversified portfolio, but he refuses to do so. If you can't sell short the company stock, you can't do the arbitrage.

The resolution of the paradox is this: yes, there are arbitrage opportunities, but not every person can exploit every arbitrage opportunity. Some are made just for you, some just for others, and some for whoever can find them. Sometimes there will be technical arbitrage opportunities that for reasons of frictions and restrictions you simply cannot trade. Does that mean arbitrage is impossible, or commonplace?

Yes. It means both.

And that means the academics and the practitioners who call for more regulation are both wrong. There should be no regulation whatsoever. Arbitrage is what happens when freedom blooms.

But we do not live in a completely free world and we do not trade in a completely free market. Thus, when pricing and hedging, we always need to be mindful of the rules and regulations governing our options, and the risk that they may change at any moment.

> "Tyranny and anarchy are never far apart."
>
> *Jeremy Bentham*

We should also keep in mind that regulations can provide their own source of arbitrage. When some institutions have regulatory reasons for trading, whether it is to increase their stakes in sub-prime mortgages or invest in politically favored industries, it is almost always a signal for a potential arbitrage opportunity to go the other way.

## 2.3  The Golden Rule of Financial Hacking

A non-Jew once approached the two leading rabbis two thousand years ago. He asked the first to teach him the whole Torah while standing on one foot; in other words, quickly. The first rabbi chased him away with a stick. (To be fair, it was a measuring stick, but still, a stick!)

The non-Jew asked the second rabbi, named Hillel. Hillel answered, and his response encoded what has come to be known as the golden rule: "What is hateful to you, do not do unto others. This is the whole Torah; the rest is commentary. Now go and study."

There are three important aspects here. First, the real Golden Rule of Hillel is not what you might usually think. He does not say to treat others as you would like them to treat you. Instead, he says to refrain from treating others as you would not like them to treat you. It is the difference between a command to do good and a command to abstain from evil. It is impossible to fulfill the duty to do good; one can always do more, and the goodness itself subjectively depends on others. But it is possible to fulfill the duty to abstain from evil: one can simply not hurt others, and the harm, if done, is more objectively noticeable.

Second, Hillel's wisdom frames all ethical knowledge and teachings around this simple principle. In this way, when details begin to confuse, as they always tend to do, one can retreat to the big picture to see how it all fits in.

Third, Hillel points out that the Golden Rule is not the end of knowledge but rather the beginning. The important thing is not what you know, but what you have yet to find out.

> "He who does not increase his knowledge decreases it."
>
> *Rabbi Hillel*

If Hillel were a trader today, and a non-trader were to ask him to teach him all there is about financial hacking while standing on one foot, I imagine Hillel might answer something like this: "Accumulate risks that are hateful to others; dispose of risks that are hateful to you. That is the whole of financial hacking; the rest is commentary. Now go and trade."

As profound as that may sound, the key part of the golden rule of financial hacking is not the first sentence, nor the second, nor the third; it is the semicolon.

> "Here is a lesson in creative writing. First rule: Do not use semicolons. They are transvestite hermaphrodites representing absolutely nothing. All they do is show you've been to college."
>
> *Kurt Vonnegut*

The poor, misunderstood semicolon. For half a millennium it has separated phrases of opposing meaning; it has also signified a connection between the statements. Where the colon announces, the semicolon hugs. In programming, the semicolon can mark the end of one thought, such as the end of a line; indicate the beginning of a comment, such as the one you are reading now; or catalog items in a list that is too complicated for the plain old comma.

That semicolon is the epitome of financial hacking. It takes two somewhat related concepts and joins them together in an uneasy alliance that is not quite as tight-knit as a comma and not quite as arms-length as a period; not quite as together as with an "and" and not quite as opposite as with a "but."

In our world, these two somewhat related concepts are fundamentally related yet relatively mispriced assets; the semicolon is the trade. It is all well and good to say these two assets ought to have the same price; how do you do actually do it?

# Chapter 3

# Trading Puzzles

Sometimes behind the simplest concepts lurk deep mysteries. If we have a good sense of what risk is, and we see what seems like a good arbitrage opportunity, we might think that actually putting on the trade would be easy, straightforward, and fun. We'd be wrong on two of those three.

## 3.1 The Price and Value of an Oracle

How much would you pay to know with absolute certainty what the closing price of the S&P 500 would be one month from today?

Not you meaning some abstract concept of an investor, but quite literally you, the reader, if you are reading this book, or the listener, if you are having it read to you. You have at your disposal the assets you actually have, your friends, your family, your credit rating. How much would you pay for this information? (And then, what would you do with it?)

> "The ancient oracle said that I was the wisest of all the Greeks. It is because I alone, of all the Greeks, know that I know nothing."
>
> *Socrates*

By way of background, the S&P 500 is an index of 500 of the most liquidly traded and largest stocks in America. It is itself a very well-traded portfolio with daily trading volume on its various futures contract accounting for billions and billions of dollars. If it helps you decide on the maximum amount you would pay for the information, let's suppose it trades $50 billion per day. And for concreteness, let's say its current price in the futures market is $1000.

Would you pay at least a dollar for this information? If your answer is no, it is likely because you think I will scam you or give you false information. It is good that you are skeptical, but for the purposes of this question, let's put that aside. If it helps, you can think of the payment as happening only conditional on the S&P 500 actually closing in a month at the price I predict today; in other words, you can pay me out of your profits. Better yet, activate your imagination or suspend your disbelief until you are able to conceive of the possibility that this is real information, real truth. It is a thought experiment.

> "There is no doubt that the thought experiment introduces the greatest transformations in our thinking and reveals the most significant paths of investigation."
>
> *Ernst Mach*, "On Thought Experiments" (1897)

To further clarify, no one else on Earth knows what the price will be. Only I know, and you are the only person I will tell, and I will not trade based on this information myself.

Okay, so you would pay at least a dollar for this information. What is the most that you would pay?

Think of me as a one-time auctioneer with a hidden reserve price. If you say a number higher than my reserve, you will receive the information. If you say a number lower, then I will tell you to go away, and we have no further dealings with each other.

In polling people on this kind of question, the usual answer is some number in the range of $1 million to $100 million. The basic thinking goes like this: I can probably put together about a million dollars if I sell everything I own, everything my family owns, and borrow to the hilt. Then I would buy or sell futures contracts and reap the leveraged benefits.

Those answering on the upper end of the scale tend to think they can successfully raise money quickly from outside investors. But this is a tough proposition. What are you going to say to investors? I know where the S&P 500 will be in one month? You have no track record, no intermediate predictions that will come true beforehand, and no sustainable business model. Anybody who hears this story and gives you money is doing so out of friendship or pity or amusement. Such people are more commonly called friends rather than investors.

Let's say you give a number like $10 million, and I accept it. The S&P 500 is currently at 1000. I gaze deeply into your eyes and tell you the truth: in one month, the S&P 500 will close that day's trading at a level of.... 1000.

Oops! Now what? How are you going to make money? You owe me $10 million in a month, and I will collect. There is no point in buying or selling futures at the same price at which you expect them to expire. So what can you do?

All you can do is hope the market moves in the meantime, and it really is a hope, because you have no other information about what is going to happen over the course of the next month, not the volatility, nor the volume, nor the highs and lows. All you know is that it will be at 1000 again a month from now.

So how do you time your entry points? Say you have $1 million of liquid assets and say that this much money would let you support up to $10 million in notional, because futures have a haircut of about 10 percent.

Suppose you are very lucky and the S&P 500 jumps down to 900 before you even have a chance to put in your order. Now you would want to buy. But how much? Do you put your entire amount on the line, such that even a single tick against you triggers a margin call from the exchange in which they ask you for more collateral, collateral that you don't have, and which then triggers a liquidation of your position?

You have to ease your way into it, and you will constantly run the risk of ending the month vindicated but penniless because it moved too far against you in the meantime. Ultimately you can perhaps do best if you are able to buy and sell options, but there won't always be a liquid options market at every strike you need at the asset that you want to trade, and besides, we haven't really discussed options yet.

These kinds of practical issues are ignored in standard textbook discussions of riskless profit opportunities but they are precisely the issues that financial hackers worry about most. And you will almost surely never experience anything with this level of certainty at any time in your career. There will always be doubts about your model, your inputs, and your forecasts.

> "Your own reason is the only oracle given you by heaven, and you are answerable for, not the rightness, but the uprightness of the decision."
>
> *Thomas Jefferson*

The problems that can occur even in such a stylized best case will be even more important when the happy assumptions of perfect, exact, and unique knowledge fade away.

## 3.2 The Difficulties of the Simplest Relative Value Trade

Pop quiz, hotshot: two fundamentally identical assets have different prices. What do you do? What do you do?

> "Interactive TV, Jack! Wave of the future — ha ha ha, huh?"
>
> Howard Payne (Dennis Hopper), the villain in *Speed* (1994)

The standard answer is to buy the cheap one and sell the expensive one, if you can, and otherwise to do nothing. For example, if it is illegal to borrow the expensive one in order to short it, or if there is simply no one willing to lend it to you, then the standard answer is to do nothing. Let the opportunity waste away.

But that's just being insufficiently creative. If the expensive asset cannot be borrowed or sold short, perhaps it is part of an index. And perhaps that index has an associated futures contract, or can serve as the basis of a swap with a counterparty. Then you can buy all the shares in the index at the correct weights and hedge your long index exposure with a short futures or a short swap on the entire index. Doing so may cost you some amount of money to carry the position, but it will give you this benefit: you will now be long the very shares you want to sell.

Since the asset is in the index with some weight, and you have replicated it when you bought the index, you can now sell long. You don't need to borrow. Another way of thinking about it is that you are borrowing from yourself. You have replicated the loan market for that asset.

These obstacles to putting on the simple relative value trade, such as an inability to borrow, are called limits to arbitrage. Anything that makes it more difficult for neutral third parties to bring prices back in line is a limit to arbitrage.

It is these limits that financial hackers must combat every day.

Almost all of these limits are external, beyond the control of the arbitrageur. The legality of borrowing. The availability of borrow. The borrow fee.

More generally, transactions costs are usually external restrictions. Commissions can only go so low. But some transactions costs can be partially controlled by the arbitrageur: slippage costs can be offset with patience and an increased risk of price movement.

For example, consider a trader who needs to buy one share of IBM where the market is 99 bid and 101 offered. He could just buy it at 101 and be done, but then his slippage is $1, the difference between the mid price in the instant before the price and the transaction price.

He could sit on the bid and hope he gets filled there, but then he takes the risk of not getting his trade done at all. As a reasonable middle ground, he could place a bid at the current mid price of 100, and have a higher likelihood of getting filled. He trades off the certainty of getting filled at 101 with the possibility of lower slippage at 100.

Now consider a trader who wants to buy the cheap A shares of a company and sell the expensive B shares. He faces twice the bid-offer spread because he would have to cross the market both times.

If he again tries to bid the A shares at mid-market to lower his slippage, then as soon as he is filled, he is virtually required to immediately cross the whole market on the short side and sell the B shares at the bid. Why?

(a) It is a legal requirement.
(b) It is a regulatory requirement.
(c) It is best practices in the industry.
(d) It is because of the risk.

The answer is (d). When the IBM trader got filled, his resulting risk profile was exactly what he wanted. In contrast, when the A/B trader was filled on his first trade, his risk profile was out of whack: he was in a queasy intermediate state between having no risk and no position and having his desired risk and his desired position. There are only two ways out of this arbitrageur's purgatory: fill the second leg to complete the relative value trade or liquidate the first leg to get out.

The A/B trader does have one advantage over the IBM trader, however: he is not as impatient to get into the trade. The IBM trader wants to go long and is merely trying to minimize his costs. The A/B trader can be a little more reflective: if he is not able to get into the trade at his desired level, he wants no part of it. If IBM moves up to 102 before the trader gets in, he will be quite sad. But if the A/B mispricing moves down a little bit before the relative value trader gets in, he will be essentially indifferent.

Another factor working in the relative value trader's favor is that the mispricing between two assets is more stationary than the price of a single asset, in the sense that the spread is more likely than the level to come back at some point to the initial value.

The usual algorithm for trading a spread is this: put mid-market orders on both sides and as soon as one is hit, move the price on the other to cross the market. In this way, you can end up paying half of the bid-offer spread on only one leg rather than on both.

When can we use this trading strategy?

(a) Only when entering into a new position.
(b) Only when exiting an existing position.
(c) Both when entering a new position or exiting an existing one.
(d) Neither when entering nor when exiting.

The most correct answer is probably (a). This strategy only works exactly as specified for entering the trade. When you have to exit, you are in more of a hurry, and you may not have the wherewithal to hold off and wait for one of your legs to be lifted at mid. In other words, you may no longer have the luxury of being indifferent in the event the trade is not done.

That said, you may simply choose to deploy the strategy in a more aggressive way by putting in order on both legs that are even more than the mid for purchases and less than the mid for sales.

In addition to borrow-related constraints and slippage and commissions costs, there are other limits to arbitrage. In a sense they are all transactions costs because they represent an additional obstacle that costs money to overcome.

But sometimes the transactions costs are not even quantifiable. If you want to trade local vs. foreign shares in a country where only natives are allowed to purchase local shares (such as Thailand), then it is not even clear how much it would cost to set up a relationship with a multinational bank having local offices in that country willing to enter into a total return swap with you to pay you the performance of the local share in exchange for a floating interest rate denominated in that country's currency. There are just too many details and moving parts to be able to know ahead of time what that will cost.

Other limits to arbitrage are more ephemeral. For example, the mere existence of noise traders may mean a pricing discrepancy can persist longer than you can sustain your position. And if you are a fund relying on outside investors, those outside investors may chase performance, and thus seek to redeem when your performance is poor, at a time when the opportunities for arbitrage are actually greatest.

Yet other limits to arbitrage need not be external at all. Self-imposed limits to arbitrage such as restrictions on maximum position size or trading activity as a portion of average daily volume are perfectly natural, commonplace in the industry, and totally in violation of academic concepts of arbitrage.

After all, if a trade presents the mispricing of a lifetime, standard theory suggests you should bet the whole farm on it. Of course, reality is not standard theory. Why is it that people and institutions voluntarily impose limits on themselves and thus fail to immediately eliminate mispricings in the market?

(a) Because of employer-employee agency problems.
(b) As a self-control mechanism.
(c) To provide for orderly liquidation if need be.

The answer is any and all of the above. Each of those reasons is sufficient by itself. In any event, those internal restrictions represent another limit to arbitrage, but rather than being something that needs to be overcome, they represent limits on how much you would choose to want to do. Nevertheless, though they still should not exist in standard definitions of arbitrage, they represent a real limitation on the amount of trading that will actually be done to eliminate a mispricing in the real world.

## 3.3 The Curious Case of HSBC

The limits to arbitrage discussed in the last chapter do not typically change very much over short periods of time. Commissions, slippage, and the borrow situation are fairly stable. Internal restrictions have inertia. Your investors are the same people today as they were yesterday. Thus, while limits to arbitrage can suggest *how much* to trade, they shed no light on the question of just *how* to trade, conditional on your desire to do so.

In the simplest example of a dual class A/B trade, where one share of the A class is supposed to be in all respects identical to one share of the B class, but the B price exceeds the A price, what are you supposed to do?

> "There may be said to be two classes of people in the world: those who constantly divide the people of the world into two classes, and those who do not."
>
> *Robert Benchley*

This is not just a hypothetical. A situation just like this actually existed from 1992 to 1999. HSBC issued a new share class that was intended to be identical in every possible respect to the old share class, from voting to dividends to liquidation rights to tax treatment to currency. They were even traded side-by-side in the same exchange in London. Both had high daily volume. Both were members of the top indices. Each was easily available to borrow and short. Analysts often wrote about how investors buying the expensive share were literally "wasting their money." Yet one of them cost more than the other. And it wasn't always the same one.

Figure 3.1 plots the relative price of the new share to the old share. The relative price is just the natural logarithm of the ratio, to express the mispricing in percentage terms.

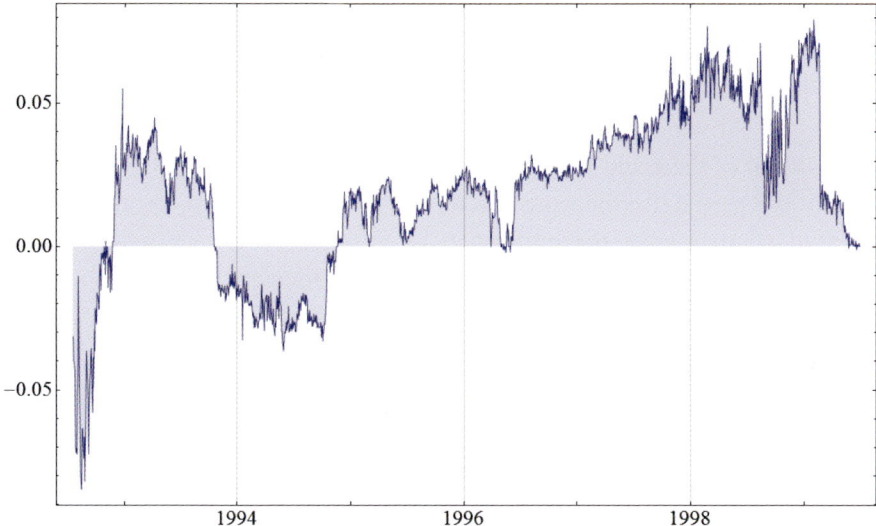

Figure 3.1. The relative price of the HSBC new share class to the old share class

Initially, the new share class was a discount of as much as eight percent. Then it inexplicably became the more expensive of the two share classes for a while, then the less expensive, until it settled into a long and final stint, with rare exceptions, of being the more expensive share class. Ultimately, the two share classes were merged one-for-one and replaced with a new single share class.

No amount of external limits to arbitrage, singly or in combination, can explain this discrepancy. Any argument you could make about investors preferring one share over the other because of minute differences in some characteristic would fail because the pricing discrepancy went both ways while the characteristics remained unchanged.

This is not a little puzzle. Over the course of the seven years that the discrepancy existed, traders committed £60 billion in capital to the more expensive share class, wasting £2 billion to do so, relative to the less expensive share class they could have bought instead. At its peak, the discrepancy represented a mispricing on HSBC of £3 billion. That's a lot of money.

If you can understand how you are supposed to trade this pair, then you will have gone a long way to understanding how to trade in general. Here are just a few items to consider.

When should you get in? And how quickly?

What is the maximum possible size trade you will do in this pair at any level? At what level will you throw up your hands, admit defeat, and just get out of the trade?

Should you exit when the discrepancy is exactly zero, or after it has crossed so that your net exit price is zero after transactions costs, or before it has crossed so that your net exit price is perhaps twice the amount of average transactions costs?

Who of your competitors are also doing this trade? Are they full up on their allocation or still loading up? Are any of them in danger of shutting down or might otherwise be interested in offloading a block trade?

According to standard theoretical concepts of arbitrage, none of those questions matters. According to real world practical experience, you can't even begin to trade until you have answered all of them.

One trick to measuring the amount of arbitrageurs already participating in a particular pairs trade is to use the concept of relative volume. Relative volume is just like relative price except instead of looking at the log ratio of prices, we look at the log ratio of volumes.

Let's say that the expensive share class was also the one that usually had more volume. This was the case with HSBC and seems to be the case generally in such trades.

Then when the relative price rises, what should happen to the relative volume?

(a) It should go up because that means even more fools are buying the expensive one.
(b) It should go down because the active fools are the ones selling the cheap one.

Neither of those are quite right. The actual answer is that the relative volume should tend to go down when the relative price goes up, but the reason is not because of noise traders or fools, but because of arbitrageurs.

Here's the logic. The relative volume is the log of the volume of the expensive share to the volume of the cheap share. When the relative price goes up, that makes the relative mispricing more attractive for arbitrageurs, so they begin trading the pair more aggressively.

When arbitrageurs trade, whether it is dollar-for-dollar or share-for-share (see next subsection), they are still trading approximately the same number of shares of each share class. So they are adding a constant to the numerator and the denominator of the relative volume, and it is the same constant.

Adding a constant to the numerator and denominator of a fraction brings it closer to one. Because we have assumed that the expensive share is the one with more volume generally, the relative volume used to be greater than one. So arbitrage activity as a result of the increased relative price pushes the relative volume down towards one.

That's why the relative price and the relative volume often appear negatively related to each other. And that is a trick few people know. You can use it to estimate the amount of arbitrage activity in the pair.

## 3.4 Dollar-for-Dollar or Share-for-Share?

The new share class of HSBC was supposed to be equivalent on a one-for-one basis with the old share class of HSBC. But their prices were different. Let's say the B shares cost $105 and the A shares cost $100 and you were able to put on the trade. How should you do it?

(a) Buy one A share for $100 and sell short one B share for $105.
(b) Buy $100 worth of the A shares and sell short $100 worth of B shares (or equivalently, buy one A share and sell 1/1.05 B shares).

This is not a question with a simple real-world answer. The academic answer is trivial of course: (a), by the definition of arbitrage. But in the real world, it is not so straightforward.

Let's say the two share classes have essentially the same betas to the market, meaning when the overall market goes up, each of the share classes reacts with the same proportional change. Specifically, let's assume the beta is one. When the market is up 10 percent, each of the share classes are also up 10 percent.

You, fresh off of the academic boat, have bought one A share and sold short one B share. You are pleased with yourself because you did exactly what academic arbitrage said to do: you found two fundamentally identical securities with different prices and you bought one and sold the other. Of course, in academia, you're never taught what to do when you wake up the next morning and the discrepancy has not disappeared.

> "When I woke up this morning, my girlfriend asked me, 'Did you sleep good?'
>
> I said, 'No, I made a few mistakes.'"
>
> *Steven Wright*

Good morning. The market is up 10 percent. It is a great day. All of your fellow traders and sales people are rejoicing because of the strong economic news that has lifted all stocks, including both of your share classes. What is the value of the discrepancy now?

The A shares rose from $100 to $110. The B shares rose from $105 to $115.50. And the value of your portfolio went down by $0.50: if you were to liquidate your position now and sell the A share and buy back the B share, you would have lost $0.50. No one else can understand why you are so inexplicably gloomy on such a bright and wonderful day, or why you get sadder and sadder the more the market goes up.

Burned once, you refuse to make the same mistake again. The next A/B share opportunity you find, you decide to hedge them dollar-for-dollar. This way, you don't care which way the market moves. It can go up or down, but the percentage discrepancy of your position will remain the same.

In the example above, the value of your A shares would have risen to $110, and the value of your B shares would have risen to $115.50. Since you bought and sold $100 of each, your net profit is zero. But, if the discrepancy ever did collapse, you would make some money. For instance, if the B share fell from $115.50 to $110, you would liquidate your position for a profit of $5.50.

What is the cost of this dollar-for-dollar trading? What is the downside? Maybe you make less money on the convergence than otherwise. But this is not true! In our example, the share-for-share profit would have always been $5, regardless of when or how the convergence occurred. But because you traded dollar-for-dollar and the market went up, you actually made more money!

Could dollar-for-dollar be a superior way of trading the discrepancy?

Not necessarily. Had the market gone down by 10 percent, and then the two share classes converged, you would have made a 10 percent smaller profit. In fact, you can think of the dollar-for-dollar trade as being exactly the same as the share-for-share trade, plus an additional long amount in the expensive share equal to the amount of the dollar discrepancy.

Specifically, with A costing $100 and B costing $105, the dollar-for-dollar position is the share-for-share position of long one share of A and short one share of B, plus a long position in 5/105 shares of B. The difference in the profit between share-for-share and dollar-for-dollar comes precisely from this net long position.

So why be long? Because of the market risk.

---

It took a long long long time

Now I'm so happy I found you

How I love you.

*The Beatles*, "Long, Long, Long" (1968)

---

If you know the convergence will happen within a few months, you are probably better off just trading it share-for-share, and taking the short-term mark-to-market risk of your portfolio moving against you in the meantime because of broad market movements.

But if you think the convergence may take years, you may be better off with the smaller daily mark-to-market profit variation, at the cost of greater terminal profit variation. With share-for-share, you know for sure what your profit will be when the two share classes merge. With dollar-for-dollar, your profit depends on the level of the market when the convergence happens. If the convergence happens when the market is low, your profit will be low.

> I shall be telling this with a sigh
> Somewhere ages and ages hence:
> Two roads diverged in a wood, and I—
> I took the one less traveled by,
> And that has made all the difference.
>
> *Robert Frost*, "The Road Not Taken"

There is one other wrinkle to the dollar-for-dollar way of trading, and that's the fact that you have to rebalance if you want to maintain your dollar-for-dollar exposure. A share-for-share trade never needs to be rebalanced, but in dollar-for-dollar, if the discrepancy widens to say $10 from $5, you need to either buy more of the A share or buy back some of the B shares to maintain an equal dollar exposure.

This additional trading can bring with it its own profit profile, one that depends neither on the overall direction of the market or the discrepancy, but on their correlation *and* on whether you are willing to increase your bet!

Say you always want to maintain a $100 exposure in each share class. Then if the discrepancy tends to widen when the market rises, you would be buying back the B shares at a high price, and selling more of them at a low price. That would hurt you over the long run.

But let's say you are willing to increase your position size. Then if the market is up and the discrepancy is wider, you can buy more of the A shares instead of the B shares. And when the market and the discrepancy come down, you can sell more of the B shares. The result will be that your overall position size is larger, but you haven't necessarily lost money yet.

There is no easy straightforward answer. There are only issues and considerations for you to weigh. That's what makes it fun!

# Part 2

# Vanilla Derivatives

# Chapter 4

# Black-Scholes

If you have an interview for a derivatives position in five minutes, and you know nothing about options, this is the chapter for you. You probably won't get the job but at least you won't look foolish. And they may simply be screening out fools in this round; you may just buy yourself enough time to learn something more before they call you back.

## 4.1 Introduction

> "All men think of themselves as kind of low level superheroes. When men are growing up and they're reading about Batman, Spiderman, Superman... these aren't fantasies. These are *options*."
>
> *Jerry Seinfeld*

There are two types of financial options: a *call* and a *put*. If you buy a call, then you own the right to purchase something at some fixed future date at some fixed price. If you buy a put, then you own the right to sell something at some fixed future date for some fixed price.

You don't have to exercise your option. It's your choice. For example, if you own a call option to buy one share of IBM for $100, but IBM is now trading at $90, then you would not exercise your option, because you could just as easily buy the same share in the market for a lower price. Why pay $100 when you could pay $90 instead?

The price of $100 on your option is called a *strike price* and we would say your option is *struck* at $100. For a call on IBM, you make money if IBM's stock price ends up above your strike price. For a put, you make money if the stock price ends up below your strike price.

44                           *Financial Hacking*

An option is *in-the-money* (ITM) if you would rather exercise it today than get nothing, *out-of-the-money* (OOTM) if you would rather get nothing than exercise it today, and *at-the-money* (ATM) if you are indifferent. For example, a call on Dell struck at $100 is ATM when Dell is at $100, ITM when Dell is at $110, and OOTM when Dell is at $90 (because you would rather get nothing than lose $10 by paying $100 for a share of Dell that only costs $90 in the market).

How do you remember these things? It will get stuck in your brain. You might have thought ATM stood for Automated Teller Machine but after even a little exposure to financial derivatives, every time you pass a bank, you will think the signs are about at-the-money options.

---

"We're in the money! We're in the money!"

*The Gold Diggers' Song* (1933)

---

If you buy options, you want them to end up in-the-money, so you can make a profit and sing that song. And how do you remember out-of-the-money? Just know that if you buy options and they end up out-of-the-money, then you are out of the running… for a bonus, a promotion, etc.

Some options are *European* and some options are *American*. European options can only be exercised at *maturity*, the date at which the option expires. American options can be exercised at any time, up to and including the maturity. How do you remember which is which? The American Revolution was fought to attain more freedom than Europe; American options give you more freedom than European ones.

Consider a European call struck at $100, with a one-year maturity, on an underlying with a current price of $120. Is it in-the-money?

(a) Yes, because you would rather exercise it than lose it for zero.
(b) No, because you can't exercise it today. It is a European option, so you can only exercise it at maturity, one year from today.

The answer is (a). It is true that you can't actually exercise the call option today. But if you could, then you would. And that is how the terms in-the-money, out-of-the-money, and at-the-money are used in the real world: moneyness is not about actual exercise, particularly in the case of European options, but about whether you would if you could. So moneyness is simply about whether the current price is above the strike for a call, or below the strike for a put.

If you have bought more of something than you have sold of it, then you are *long* it, and if you sold more of something than you have bought of it, then you are *short* it.

This is true for any financial security or contract. Net buyers are long and net sellers are short.

So if you are long an option, whether it is a put or a call, your worst-case loss is:

(a) Zero.
(b) Whatever you paid for the option.
(c) Your entire capital.
(d) Infinity — you could end up in debt forever.

The answer is none of the above. If you just bought the option, and you bought it at a fair price, without any markup, then the answer is (b), whatever you paid for the option. But in general, the answer is whatever the current market price is.

Like any asset with limited liability (meaning, a security that can't be worth less than zero) that is marked to its fair market price (meaning, the security is revalued or reassessed periodically to an estimate of what it would sell for in the market), you stand to lose its market value, and no more.

But the market price is not necessarily what you paid for it originally. If you bought an option for $6 and it now costs $4, the most you can lose as of today is only $4. Your original purchase price for the option doesn't matter. Those two dollars are already gone forever; it is a sunk cost. And what if the price comes back up to $6? Then that will be a new $2 you have made.

The option will always have some price.

If it doesn't, then you should buy as much of it as you can, once you make sure you are really buying an option and not selling one. A free option is *pure arbitrage*, meaning riskless profit. Even if the option expires worthless, you have lost nothing. It's like getting a free lottery ticket.

What if you are short an option? What is your worst-case loss?

(a) Zero.
(b) Whatever money I received for selling the option.
(c) The option's current market value.
(d) The strike price times the number of options I sold.
(e) Infinity.

Surprise! There is no single correct answer. The answer is (d) for puts and (e) for calls. If you sold 50 put options struck at $100 on Microsoft, the worst case for you happens when Microsoft becomes worthless, i.e., has a price of zero, and whoever you sold the option to chooses to exercise it, forcing you to buy 50 shares of Microsoft at $100 each. In that case, you would lose 50 times 100, or $5,000. Microsoft can't go below zero, so that is your worst-case loss for a short put. But if you sold 50 call options struck at $100 on Microsoft, then if Microsoft goes up to $1,100, you would lose $50,000; if Microsoft soars to $10,100, you would lose $500,000; and so on. You could in theory lose an infinite amount of money by selling calls.

Of course, people set up limited liability entities for trading, so that the most they can lose is their capital.

Most importantly, so far we have been talking only about *naked* option selling, meaning selling options without any *hedging*. Hedging means making trades to reduce your risk. Just like landscapers trim bushes and hedges so that the only greenery that's left is the one they want, so too do traders hedge away all of the unwanted risk so that the only exposure that's left is the one they want.

> "Whoso breaketh an hedge, a serpent shall bite him."
>
> *Ecclesiastes 10:8*

There are three important numbers associated with each option that unfortunately all start with the letter $p$, but they are very different, so you have to memorize them well.

The amount of money you pay initially to buy an option, or the amount of money you collect initially to sell an option, is called the *premium*. Think of it like premium super unleaded gasoline: you always have to pay first at the pump before you can fill your tank.

> "Stop! That's my car! Hey, that smells like regular. She needs premium, dude! PREMIUM! DUUUUUDE!!"
>
> *Snake*, lamenting L'il Bandit, "The Simpsons" (1997)

The amount of money you will make on your option is called its *payoff*, and it is unknown when you first make the trade. Think of it like the payoff in a bank robbery. You don't know what it will be at the time you start the heist. You only find out once you actually get inside the vault.

> "Who would have guessed reading and writing would pay off!"
>
> *Homer*, "The Simpsons" (1991)

Finally, the amount of money you will have made at the end, minus whatever it cost you, is your *profit*. That's easy. But remember that you always have to compare dollars at the same time as each other. You paid a premium a long time ago and just got your payoff today. To calculate your profit, you have to find today's value of your premium, which usually just means adjusting for the interest it earned or cost you in the meantime.

> "I tell ya, I'm a financial genius. I buy an eight-dollar lobster, fatten it into an 80-dollar lobster, and eat the profits!"
>
> *Homer*, "The Simpsons" (1998)

In general, your option doesn't have to be on IBM or Dell or Microsoft, or even on a stock at all. It could be on a bond or on a currency or on anything else. Whatever it is on is called the *underlying* — quite naturally, because it *underlies* the option security. The term underlying actually applies to any derivative, not just options, but it turns out that just about all derivatives can be expressed as a combination of options, and, as we are about to see, even a put can be expressed in terms of a call, and vice versa.

## 4.2 Put-Call Parity

A common interview question is: "Can you prove the put-call parity?"

As with much of finance, there are two ways of proving it. One is a mathematical approach that focuses on details such as the interest rate, the dividends of the underlying, the particular maturity, and the compounding frequency of debt. The proof is not particularly long but it is easy to accidentally write a plus sign instead of a minus sign somewhere by accident and get confused.

On the other hand, the financial hacking proof is quick, visual, and insightful. Furthermore, it immediately suggests the exact calculations you need to do if you need additional details, with little chance of accidentally changing a sign, in the rare situation where the intuition is not enough. The financial hacking approach starts by visualizing options.

Whenever you hear the word "call," you should always visualize this:

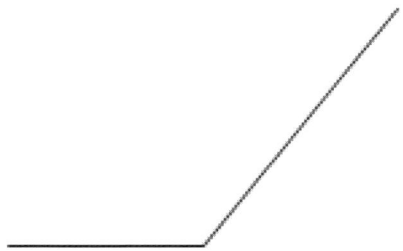

Figure 4.1. Payoff diagram of a call option

If you are right handed, you might notice that the *payoff diagram* of a call looks like a half-opened cell phone, as if you are placing a call.

What is a payoff diagram? It is a plot of the payoff of a derivative as a function of the final underlying price.

In Figure 4.1, the payoff of a call is zero for all final underlying prices below the strike, and starts increasing for final underlying prices above the strike.

(A payoff diagram could depend on something else, but that would be explicitly specified.)

Whenever you hear the word "put," you should always visualize this:

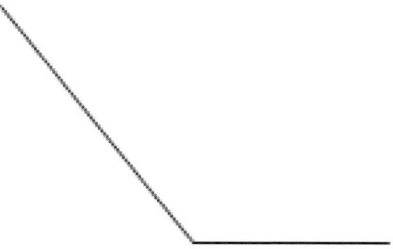

Figure 4.2. Payoff diagram of a put option

If you are right handed, you might see a golf club: specifically, a putter.

Payoff diagrams are typically plotted for the holder of the derivative. To figure out the payoff from being short either of those, flip the picture.

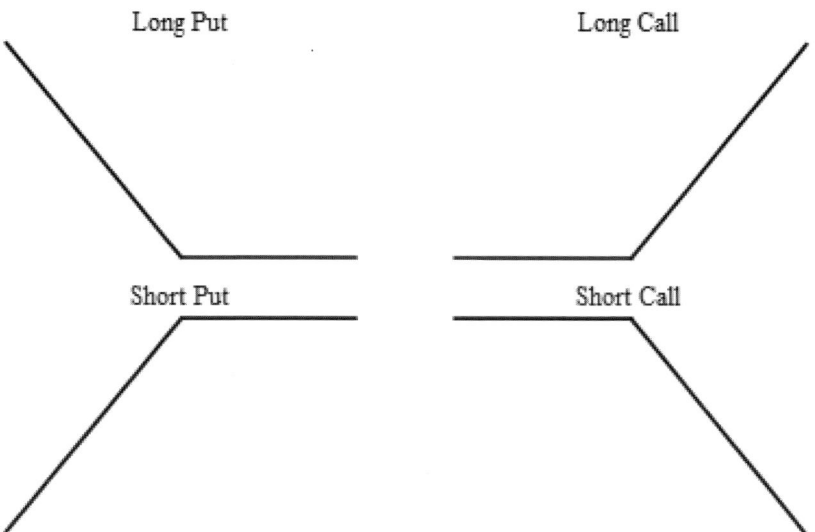

Figure 4.3. Payoff diagrams of long and short put and call options

In general, if you want to recall the payoff diagram of a long or short put or call, first remember what it looks like long, and then flip it if it is actually short.

What does all this have to do with proving put-call parity? Everything.

What's more, remembering these little diagrams will let you reconstruct more complicated options strategies such as bear spreads, bull spreads, butterflies, and others.

Let's do that first.

### 4.2.1 *Options strategies and combinations*

There are dozens of different named options combinations and an infinite amount of possibilities.

For example, if you buy a call and sell another call at a higher strike, then you have what is known as a *bull spread*. It looks like the following:

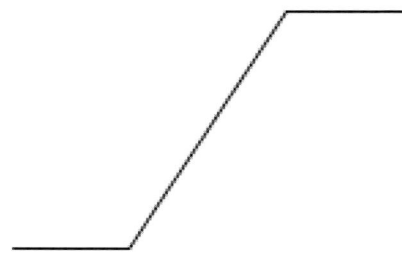

Figure 4.4. The payoff diagram of a bull spread options combination

How do you know that a couple of calls with different strikes could replicate a bull spread? Because you remember the shape of a long call and a short call and you can see that putting them together and adding them up generates the exact same graph.

What does it mean to "add up" graphs? Simple: if one is flat but the other increases, the sum increases. If one increases and the other decreases at the same rate, the sum is flat.

Could you replicate a bull spread with puts instead of calls? Sure, just look at the top right of Figure 4.4. Compare that with the short put of

Figure 4.3. Looks like the same thing, right? But the bottom left part of Figure 4.4 needs to end somehow, whereas a short put just keeps going down and to the left. So you need to taper it off with a long put with a strike at the lower kink. Done.

The payoff diagram of a bear spread is shown below:

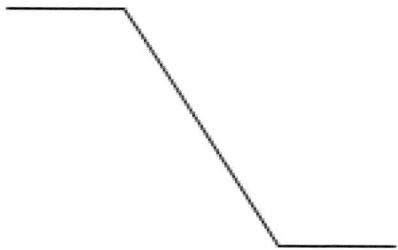

Figure 4.5. The payoff diagram of a bear spread options combination

A bear spread can be replicated with:

(a) A short call struck at the leftmost kink and a long call struck at the rightmost kink.
(b) A short put struck at the leftmost kink and a long put struck at the rightmost kink.

The answer is yes. Either way would work. Imagine the combinations in your head to see if it makes sense. The one with the calls is easy, because the individual payoff diagrams just line up. But the one with the puts seems hard, until you try this little trick: try the obvious ones first. Start with the rightmost kink. That's obviously a long put. But we need to taper it off at the left, so let's short a put at the left kink. Done.

Those kinks in the payoff diagrams are the essence of optionality. Without them, there would be no dynamic hedging, no Black-Scholes pricing model, and no volatility trading. By fiddling with the kinks, you can create *any* payout diagram. Consider the payoff diagram of a butterfly strategy:

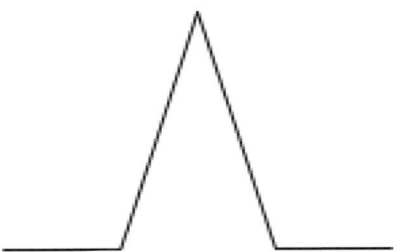

Figure 4.6. Payoff diagram of a butterfly options combination

It is called a butterfly because it sort of looks like it has wings, but it should really be called a nose. Actual butterflies found in nature are reputedly much prettier.

One way to replicate a butterfly options combination is to buy one call at the lower strike, sell two calls at the middle strike (the tip of the nose), and buy one call at the higher strike.

You can make the nose thinner by putting the strikes closer together. But that would also make the nose shorter. To make the nose thin and long, you have to increase the number of options you are buying and selling so that the slope of the nose is steeper. This is just a matter of scaling the butterfly.

You could eventually make the payoff of a thin-nosed butterfly be some fixed dollar amount if the underlying price is within 0.000001 (or any other arbitrarily small threshold) of some particular number, and zero otherwise.

But if you can do that, then you can do anything, because any payoff can be expressed as a collection of thin-nosed butterflies with particular positions, since you can lengthen any nose by buying and selling some multiple of the required number of options, and you can put a nose anywhere you need a particular dollar amount for the payoff.

So any payoff diagram can be replicated with just plain-vanilla calls and puts.

> "Ah, you flavour everything; you are the vanilla of society."
>
> *Sydney Smith*

## 4.2.2 Replicating forwards

One particular payoff diagram is that of a *forward* contract.

Unlike a call option, which gave you the right to buy at a future date for a fixed price, a forward obligates you to buy at a future date for a fixed price. See also Chapter 1.

So being long a forward at a fixed strike price is just like being long a call and short a put at the same strike price, because if the underlying ends up above the strike, you would choose to exercise your call and buy the underlying at the strike price, and if the underlying ends up below the strike, whoever you sold the put to would choose to exercise it and force you to buy the underlying at the strike price.

Either way, you will buy the underlying at the strike price at maturity, just as you would with a forward.

The easiest way to see this is with Figure 4.7.

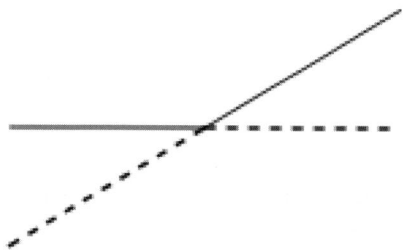

Figure 4.7. The payoff diagram of a long call (solid) and a short put (dashed)

The combination of a long call and a short put aggregates into a simple straight line, equal to the payoff diagram of a forward with the same strike as the put and call.

That's basically the entire put-call parity. So much easier than memorizing the formula. And what is that formula anyway? You can reconstruct it from the picture. The price of a call at strike $K$ minus the price of a put at the same strike $K$ equals the price of a forward at that same strike $K$:

$$C(K) - P(K) = F(K) \qquad (4.1)$$

This is true for any strike $K$. In other words, you can replicate any forward with calls and puts of the same strike price.

And what is the value of a forward contract struck at $K$? You can replicate that with some arbitrage thinking. If you are long a forward contract struck at $K$, meaning you will give up $\$K$ and receive one share of stock at maturity, and you want to hedge it, then you need to sell the stock and borrow the present value of the cash today. You would also have to pay out any dividends the stock issues along the way.

Why do you have to pay out the dividends? Because you borrowed the shares you sold from someone else. And you have to make the lender whole, so that they continue to receive the dividends they were expecting to get. In the real world, you would also have to pay them a fee for the privilege of borrowing their shares.

So that means the value of a forward is the current spot price, minus the present value of the dividends to be paid from now until maturity, minus the present value of $\$K$.

Or as a formula:

$$F(K) = S - PV(K) - PV(D)$$

And so we have derived the put-call parity formula that:

$$C(K) - P(K) = S - PV(K) - PV(D)$$

Try this experiment. Read a few more pages and then try to write down the put-call parity formula from memory. Chances are you will get at least one of the signs wrong. Many people do. If you are being interviewed and asked about the put-call parity, you are likely to make a mistake as well.

But if you just recall the pretty pictures, you will get all of the intuition and none of the risk of misplaced minus signs. Plus you will always be able to re-derive the formula correctly.

### 4.2.3 The big lessons of the put-call parity

But wait, you say. What is so important about the put-call parity, anyway? Technically, it is nothing more than the description and pictures above, that a long call plus a short put equals a forward, or, equivalently, that a call is a put plus a forward. It is just about how puts and calls relate to each other. But intuitively, it is much more.

The big intuitive insight from put-call parity is that it doesn't matter whether you trade in puts or in calls: the two are in some deep sense identical, despite their surface differences.

Optionality is the key.

The kink is the key.

Once you have a kink, you can go long or short and you can fiddle with forwards to make it go up or down or left or right as you see fit.

Fundamentally, there is no difference between puts and calls, and this insight itself is not dependent on a particular model or restricted to only particular parameter values. It is a deep truth.

In the derivatives world, there's no such thing as a call trader or a put trader; there are only options traders.

## 4.3 Derivation of the Black-Scholes PDE

The only question more common or more valuable on an interview besides the put-call parity is this one: "Please derive the Black-Scholes PDE." PDE stands for partial differential equation.

This is the *only* part of financial hacking that looks like financial math. Still, it is just five lines of math, each of which is dense with valuable intuition. And the derivation introduces so many important concepts in such an integrated way that it would be vital to learn even if it weren't one of the most common interview questions.

If you understand this derivation deeply, you understand the basics of nearly every aspect of finance, including arbitrage, risk management, valuation, hedging, Itō's lemma, short selling, mergers, market microstructure, portfolio management, yield curves, hedge funds, behavioral finance, and more.

And all this in just five short equations.

Let's begin by acknowledging that in finance, there are no *true* models.

> "Essentially, all models are wrong, but some are useful."
>
> George E.P. Box and Norman R. Draper (1987)

So models are false, but reality is even worse: it is useless.

One useless reality is that a stock's price change is equal to its expected price change plus its unexpected price change. This is circularly true and it doesn't even depend on what specific expectation you had of its price change. Whatever expectation you had, the actual price change equaled that, plus a residual or unexpected amount, which could possibly be negative. There is no way for that statement to be false, because it is essentially just the definition of unexpected price change. But is there a way we can transform that statement into something useful?

Yes, in a model.

In other words, yes, if we make some assumptions.

Assumptions are false but useful beliefs, like the idea that the sun will come up tomorrow. No matter how many times it has happened, it's never guaranteed. But it's useful to plan our lives and record our favorite television shows.

> "Never assume the obvious is true."
>
> William Safire

The assumptions we make in finance essentially just try to formalize in as simple a way as possible our intuitive concepts. For example, how can we formalize the basic concepts of expected and unexpected price change?

One simple way is this. Let's assume that the expected price change is some proportion of the previous price, where the proportion is a constant annual drift multiplied by the exact amount of time elapsed, expressed as a portion of a year. And let's assume that the unexpected price change is some scaled white noise.

Then we have:

$$dS = \mu S dt + \sigma S dw \qquad (4.2)$$

where $dS$ is the small change in the price $S$, $\mu$ is the annualized drift of the stock (for example, something like 10 percent), $dt$ is the small change in time $t$, $\sigma$ is what we will call the *volatility* of the stock, but basically it is the annualized standard deviation of the stock return, and $dw$ is a random white noise.

Remember that here we are interested not in financial mathematical rigor but in useful financial hacking. We want to focus on everything you need to know in order to deeply understand the intuition.

The two most important insights are that:

(1) the white noise $dw$ is basically like the square root of $dt$, and
(2) $(dt)^n = 0$ for any exponent $n > 1$.

The first insight follows because random white noise has independent increments with variance proportional to the elapsed time. That means its standard deviation is proportional to the square root of the elapsed time. The elapsed time when looking at things on a continuous basis is just $dt$. So $dw$ is basically the square root of $dt$.

The second insight follows because, when $dt$ is less than one, its square root is a larger number. So we need to take $dw$'s into account. We even need to take $(dw)^2$ into account, because that is like $dt$. But everything at a higher power than $dt$? That's too small.

> "It's a small world, but I wouldn't want to have to paint it."
>
> *Steven Wright*

These two insights are the basis of what is known as Itō's lemma, which explicitly states what the dynamics of $V(S,t)$ will be for any function $V$ of the underlying price $S$ and the time $t$.

But we can derive it at a moment's notice, and under the pressure of an interview or a pending trade if need be, with some intuitive and easy-to-remember shorthand.

We are no longer at the mercy of our flawed memories. Instead we will have the tools of intuition at our fingertips to command.

Let's begin.

First, let's recall that there are three kinds of $d$'s:

(1) There is the Greek $\Delta$ (pronounced delta), meaning a small change. We might say $\Delta t$ is a small change in time, like an hour or a day.
(2) There is the lower-case $d$, meaning either a very small and essentially unnoticeable change, so that $dt$ is on the order of a millisecond, or it can mean a total derivative, like $d(x^2) = 2xdx$.
(3) Finally, there is the partial $\partial$, meaning a partial derivative, holding all other inputs constant.

> "The witty Dean Swift once wrote:
>
> > So, Nat'ralists observe, a Flea
> > Hath smaller Fleas that on him prey.
> > And these have smaller Fleas to bite 'em,
> > And so proceed ad infinitum.
>
> An ox might worry about a flea of ordinary size — a small creature of the first order of smallness. But he would probably not trouble himself about a flea's flea; being of the second order of smallness, it would be negligible. Even a gross of fleas' fleas would not be of much account to the ox."
>
> *Silvanus Phillips Thompson*, "Calculus Made Easy" (1914)

Equation (4.2) defines the *dynamics* of $S$. What would be the dynamics of $V$, which is itself a function of $S$ and $t$? To figure it out, we just take the total derivative of $V(S, t)$, which means taking the sum of each of the partial derivatives:

$$dV = \frac{\partial V}{\partial S} dS + \frac{\partial V}{\partial t} dt + \frac{1}{2} \frac{\partial^2 V}{\partial S^2} dS^2 \qquad (4.3)$$

We ignore all higher-order terms because of the rule that everything smaller than $dt$, like $dt^2$, is for all intents and purposes zero. But remember well that $dw^2 = dt$.

What is $dS^2$, the final term in Equation (4.3)? There are four cross products in $dS * dS$, all but one of them involving $dt$ times either a $dw$ or another $dt$, meaning that the result would be either $dt^{3/2}$ or $dt^2$, which are both zero. The only non-zero term is the one involving the square of the white noise term; thus $dS^2 = \sigma^2 S^2 dt$.

Let's bring the first term on the right hand side in Equation (4.3) over to the left hand side, and let's plug in the value of $dS^2$:

$$dV - \frac{\partial V}{\partial S} dS = \left( \frac{\partial V}{\partial t} + \frac{1}{2} \sigma^2 S^2 \frac{\partial^2 V}{\partial S^2} \right) dt \qquad (4.4)$$

So far this is not particularly magical. After all, we just did a total derivative and rearranged some terms. But here is where we can take a mathematical shortcut and also throw in an important financial insight.

There are actually two notations for mathematical derivatives, both rooted in the history of calculus. Isaac Newton and Gottfried Leibniz both claim to have invented calculus, but with different notation. Newton's notation involves putting dots on top of symbols, so something like $\dot{x}$ to denote the first derivative of $x$. Leibniz's notation uses little $d$'s in front of the variables, so something like $dx$ to denote the derivative of $x$. We primarily use Leibniz's notation today in almost all areas where mathematical derivatives matter.

The beauty of the $d$-like notation is that it almost seems as if we can just "factor out" the $d$'s. And in our case, we can. So we can rewrite the left hand side of Equation (4.4) with the $d$ seemingly factored out on the left:

$$d\left( V - \frac{\partial V}{\partial S} S \right) = \left( V - \frac{\partial V}{\partial S} S \right) r dt \qquad (4.5)$$

Where did the new right hand side of Equation (4.5) come from? From the following bit of financial logic: note from the right hand side of Equation (4.4) that there is no $dw$ term. What does that mean?

In general, when we see the dynamics of an asset or a portfolio that does not have a $dw$ term, what are we to infer?

In our model, the only risk is in the white noise. We specifically defined the unexpected price change to be proportional to $dw$. If there is no white noise, there is no unexpected price change, and so there is no risk.

Therefore, we have a riskless portfolio. How much should a riskless portfolio earn? The riskless amount: it should earn the riskfree rate $r$ multiplied by the amount of time elapsed $dt$ multiplied by the initial value of the security.

In other words, if you think of the stuff in parenthesis on the left hand side in Equation (4.5) as being a portfolio $\Pi$ of its own, which it is, then the change in value of that portfolio must equal its initial value times the riskfree rate times the elapsed time, i.e. $d\Pi = \Pi r dt$.

But the left hand side of Equation (4.5) is equal to the left hand side of Equation (4.4), so the two respective right hand sides must be equal too. So we can eliminate the common $dt$'s and rearrange terms to get:

$$\frac{\partial V}{\partial t} + \frac{1}{2}\sigma^2 S^2 \frac{\partial^2 V}{\partial S^2} + \frac{\partial V}{\partial S} rS - rV = 0 \qquad (4.6)$$

which is the Black-Scholes PDE.

You are done. You derived it.

For extra credit, you can rewrite it like this:

$$\Theta + \frac{1}{2}\sigma^2 S^2 \Gamma + \Delta rS - rV = 0$$

where $\Theta = \partial V/\partial t$ (theta) is the time decay, $\Gamma = \partial^2 V/\partial S^2$ (gamma) is the convexity of the derivative with respect to the underlying price, and $\Delta = \partial V/\partial S$ (delta) is the hedging ratio, the number of shares you need to sell (see Equation 4.5) in order to create a riskless portfolio.

You can also refer to the product $\Delta \cdot S$ as "dollar delta" and the product $\Gamma \cdot S^2$ as "dollar gamma." Perhaps better names would be "notional delta" and "notional gamma," but that's not what's caught on. People still tend to call it dollar delta and dollar gamma even if the underlying currency is not US dollars.

### 4.3.1 *The biggest insight from the Black-Scholes PDE*

The biggest insight is not actually there. The biggest insight is what's missing. What part of Equation (4.2) is missing in Equation (4.6)?

> "Is there any point to which you would wish to draw my attention?"
> "To the curious incident of the dog in the night-time."
> "The dog did nothing in the night-time."
> "That was the curious incident," remarked Sherlock Holmes.
> 
> *Sir Arthur Conan Doyle*, "Silver Blaze" (1892)

If you said the drift term $\mu$, you are correct.

What happened to it? Where did it go?

If you look back over the five-step derivation of the Black-Scholes PDE, you will notice that the drift term $\mu$ never comes up again. Did we make a mistake? Did we accidentally replace it with the riskfree rate $r$?

One of the most common mistakes that even highly experienced practitioners make is to act as if the assumptions of Black-Scholes (lognormal, continuous distribution of returns, no transactions costs, etc.) mean that we can always arbitrarily assume the underlying grows at the riskfree rate $r$ instead of a subjective guess as to its real drift $\mu$. But this is not quite accurate.

The insight from the Black-Scholes PDE is that the price of a *hedged* derivative does not depend on the drift of the underlying. The price of an *unhedged* derivative, for example, a naked long call, most certainly does depend on the drift of the underlying.

Let's say you are naked long an at-the-money one-year call on Apple, and you will never hedge. And suppose Apple has very low volatility. Then the only way you will profit is if Apple's drift is positive: if it drifts down, your option expires worthless.

But if you hedge the option with Apple shares, then you no longer care what the drift is. You only make money on a long option if volatility is higher than the initial price of the option predicted.

Under the assumptions of the Black-Scholes model, traders with opposite opinions about a stock's drift will still agree on the price of an option — if they agree on the stock's volatility.

Do you deeply understand this insight? Consider a Black-Scholes world where the risk free rate is zero. Which option should cost more: a 1-year at-the-money European put on a non-dividend-paying stock with 10% expected return and 20% volatility, or a 1-year at-the-money European call on a non-dividend-paying stock with 20% expected return and 10% volatility?

(a) The put should cost more.
(b) The call should cost more.
(c) They should have the same price.
(d) It depends on which stock's returns have higher kurtosis.
(e) It depends on which stock's returns have lower skewness.
(f) There is insufficient information to answer this question.

The only correct answer is (a) because the only thing that matters is the volatility. Even if you do not expect to hedge the option, the price in the market will likely be set by arbitrageurs who will hedge.

### 4.3.2 What else is missing from the PDE?

We know that the drift of the underlying is missing from the Black-Scholes PDE, and we now know why. But what else is "missing" from the PDE?

It has some Greeks in it — things like theta and delta and gamma. But where is rho, the sensitivity of the derivative to changes in the risk free rate? Where is vega, the sensitivity of the derivative to changes in the volatility?

Did we make a mistake somewhere in the derivation? After all, vega is perhaps the single most important Greek, after delta, of course. If options are all about volatility, and vega is a measure of the sensitivity to volatility, shouldn't vega be somewhere in the PDE?

No, it shouldn't. The PDE is the result of a model, and that model assumed a constant volatility, and a constant risk free rate. Vega and rho, respectively, measure the change in the model output price when we change the input parameter. Parameter Greeks like vega and rho are fundamentally different from sensitivity Greeks like delta and theta. They are far more important.

Sensitivity Greeks are simultaneous outputs from the model. They are supplemental information to go along with the model price. If you think of the model as a person, then the model price is its body, and the model sensitivity Greeks are its accentuating makeup and jewelry and clothes. The model is proud to calculate and display them for you. The underlying will bounce around; time will pass; the model knows this and happily exhibits your sensitivities to those events.

But parameter Greeks are an embarrassment to the model. They are the cracks beneath the makeup, the scars beneath the clothes, the hollowness inside the body. They expose the fact that the model is false.

The model refuses to calculate these directly. It denies they even exist. Essentially the only way to calculate them is to kill the model and create a new one, with new parameters, and look at the differences. Is it taller? Is its smile wider? Do its eyes sparkle more?

> "Keep cool, Simpson. Be *in* the game, but not *of* the game."
>
> *Bart Simpson*

In the real world, of course, you can insist that the computer calculate the new model values for you, but if the computer had a soul, then it would do these calculations only grudgingly. Parameter Greeks humiliate the model by reminding it that it is not special or unique in any way.

Yet these parameter Greeks like rho and vega are the most important ones, because they let you step out beyond the model. They let you measure your exposure to your uncertainty about the correct parameters to the model.

It's like buying a brand new car. The car will tell you certain things about itself. It has an odometer and a fuel indicator and many other gauges. Some even report the air pressure in the tyres. But it won't tell you what would happen if there was sudden flooding on the roads or an accident up ahead. Yet those are questions that you as an operator need to ask. And the only way you can find out, for a general kind of model, is to try it out, either for real or through simulations.

In some special cases, such as the Black-Scholes formula, you can compute closed-form expressions for these parameter Greeks.

But don't let that fool you. You are still exploring things that are outside of the model.

And it is precisely because they are outside of the model that these Greeks are so critical to risk management: if the model was correct, you wouldn't need much risk management at all.

# Chapter 5

# Simulation

To really understand a model, you have to go beyond its formal definition and derivation and actually simulate its assumptions and test its predictions. Simulations let you touch and taste the various implications of the model and develop intuition about when the model is useful and when it needs to be corrected.

## 5.1 Introduction

Think of the Black-Scholes option pricing formula as a black box. How can we tell if it is a good black box, a good model? How can we be sure it prices options correctly?

> "A good model can advance fashion by ten years."
> *Yves Saint Laurent*

This is a more important question than just confirming Black-Scholes itself. In general, every financial firm has its own peculiar version of an option pricing model, and if you are to be a trader or a quant or in any way associated with that model, you will at some point need to check if it is a good model.

You will become a more valuable person if you know its weaknesses and faults. So how can you determine that? In the same way that we will now poke at the black box of Black-Scholes options pricing.

### 5.1.1 *Ability to fit to market prices*

One quick possibility for testing a black box of any kind is to compare it to market prices. The model prices certainly do not have to match exactly (it would be weird if they did) but if they deviate systematically, then perhaps there is an important risk or parameter that the model misses. The market doesn't always need to be right, but it's almost certainly not the case that the market is always wrong.

If the model prices simply can't match the market prices, no matter what, the model is probably not a very good one. It is not likely to be very useful.

The Black-Scholes model is useful. It can match any reasonable market price. Indeed, the biggest use of the Black-Scholes model is not to calculate the model price, but to use the market price to calculate the Black-Scholes *implied volatility*. The implied volatility is the number that, when used as the input volatility in the Black-Scholes option pricing formula, generates the market price.

Model parameters that are implied from market prices are often easier to have an intuition about than are the market prices themselves, especially if the model is itself intuitive. Consider: which intuitively sounds more mispriced, an option that costs $0.05 or an option that has an implied volatility of 5 percent?

A pure financial mathematician would throw up his hands and declare insufficient information: we don't know the strike or the maturity or even the type (put or call) of the option under discussion. If pressed, the mathematician will say either one could be mispriced: the true price of the option could just as easily be $0.04 or $0.06 and the true underlying volatility could just as easily be 4 percent or 6 percent.

A financial hacker has a much simpler response. A financial hacker would immediately note that, while possible, underlyings very rarely tend to have a 5 percent or lower volatility. On the other hand, there are lots of options that cost $0.05 or less: just go out far enough on the wings for any underlying and any maturity and you will eventually find options selling for $0.05.

An experienced financial hacker would also note that the bid-offer spread of such a low-priced option tends to be a greater percentage of its price than for a higher-priced option, so the likelihood of being able to capitalize on a mispricing when the option costs $0.05 is even lower.

In short, being told that an option has a particular price means nearly nothing, but being told that an option has a particular implied volatility gives a sense of meaning to it, something that can be pondered, something on which an opinion could be formed and a trade proposed.

That is the power of model parameters. The idea is not that the model is correct, or that the assumptions can never be violated, but simply that the model is useful in explaining the risks.

The parameters help the intuition. Often the right intuition is that the market price is basically correct, more or less, and if the model is physically unable, for any intuitively reasonable choice of parameters, to match the market price, then it is a bad model. Why? Because it is not useful.

The Black-Scholes model is a very good model — not because it is right, but because it, and its parameters, are useful.

But this is a very weak test, and only the first test we need to apply to any arbitrary black box model to gauge its value.

## 5.1.2 *Internal consistency*

The next test is to see if the black box is at least internally consistent.

Every model depends on certain assumptions. A hedging model also tells you what trades you need to do every day after you put on a position — with the Black-Scholes model, the most important hedge is neutralizing the delta of the derivative with an offsetting position in the underlying.

So what if we simulate paths for the underlying exactly in accordance with the assumptions required by the model and hedge exactly as the model specifies? What will be the resulting profit or loss from buying and hedging a derivative? If it's not exactly zero, something must be amiss, either with the model or with our simulation.

Let's consider a concrete example. Say we buy an at-the-money call, then randomly simulate a single path for the underlying security with lognormal returns having constant volatility. Along that path, we will hedge our delta to the model-computed delta with the same constant volatility. This means we will be net neutral delta as far as the model is concerned. In other words, we will do exactly what Black-Scholes says we ought to do, in a Black-Scholes world, on a plain vanilla option. Then we will do the same thing across lots of different randomly simulated paths.

The question is: how much money will you make across all those different simulated paths?

(a) You will always make $0 exactly.
(b) You will make $0 on average, but not on every path.

The essence of the question is: does the model predict perfect replication, or just an average result?

As an illustration, here is a model for pricing any stock in the Dow Jones Industrial Average (DJIA, or Dow), which is a major American equity index comprising 30 blue-chip stocks: the return over the next one year for any component of the Dow will be the same as the return for the Dow itself. For example, IBM is a member of the Dow. This toy model predicts that the return on IBM will be the same as the return on the Dow over the next one year.

Obviously, IBM could go up more or less than the Dow over the next one year. It is clearly not the case that the return of IBM and the return of the Dow are always guaranteed to be exactly identical in one year's time.

But across all of the stocks in the Dow, it is true that on average, the return will be the same as the Dow. Why? Because the return on the Dow is essentially the average of the returns of its components.

Do you buy that argument? It is straightforward, but let me now try to argue you out of it. (Financial hackers often play devil's advocate. It's a great way to build deeper intuition than your competitors.)

I argue that there is a way in which this model results in a world where the return of IBM will *always* exactly equal the return of the Dow, not just on average, but on every single path. To see how, let's extend the notion of hedging from options theory to this toy model.

If we were to hedge our exposure to IBM after a few days in which IBM outperformed the Dow, we would sell IBM and buy the Dow. Why?

Because we know that the two will converge in the future, at least as far as the model goes.

For example, if IBM has risen by five percent with the Dow unchanged, we know that by the end of the year, according to the model, that difference must go to zero; in other words, the Dow will outperform IBM by five percent, or, equivalently, IBM will underperform the Dow by five percent, in the remaining time. Therefore, we can make more money by replacing our holding of IBM with a holding in the Dow.

In fact, you might imagine that if everybody believed this model, then the trading activity of hedgers would cause it to actually come true. Whenever IBM outperformed the Dow, traders would sell IBM and buy the Dow, in the process lowering the price of IBM and raising that of the Dow, until ultimately the two were in line. If everybody thought that others believed this model, and so everybody traded to it, it would become reality. This would then be an example of what Robert K. Merton (who is effectively the grandfather of continuous time finance because his son Robert C. Merton was the father) called a self-fulfilling prophecy: a false definition evoking a new behavior that causes the originally false definition to come true.

> "The specious validity of the self-fulfilling prophecy perpetuates a reign of error."
>
> *Robert K. Merton* (1948)

How strong is my argument that in a world where everybody believed the toy model, the model would alter reality and all stocks would have identical returns? Not very, the reason being that there will eventually be arbitrage limits. If a company has truly had great performance and is now stockpiling cash, hedgers would initially keep its return and hence its price low, but at some point, the amount of net cash in the firm would exceed its market capitalization, so that a single person could buy the firm and liquidate it for a substantial profit. When you can liquidate immediately, you don't care what model others believe in.

In general, it can be difficult at times to decide how to behave or how to properly hedge when you believe the market is wrong. We will return to this question later, when we examine the concept of hedging to market versus hedging to model. The answer will depend on the same issues raised in this toy model.

Thus there ought not be a self-fulfilling prophecy with this toy model. And so the model will only be correct on average. There will be paths in which IBM outperforms model expectations and paths where it underperforms model expectations.

Options pricing models are supposed to be different. There, you are supposed to make a fixed and guaranteed amount of profit on every single path, because there is no risk involved, at least in theory.

We could check the internal consistency of that theory by simulating many option paths to see if the profit is indeed exactly zero on every possible path.

## 5.2 Simulation

How do we simulate a single path in a Black-Scholes world? The first problem we run into is our discrete world. Black-Scholes assumes continuous time but our computers can only store a finite amount of digits and numbers.

Your first thought for a suggestion is indeed the natural solution: just simulate it with pretty small time steps of say a day or an hour or a second in duration. If using such reasonably small time steps causes Black-Scholes to fail, then the model must not be very useful, since reality, especially financial reality, is far more discrete than it is continuous.

Okay, so how exactly do we simulate a single time step? What parameters should we use?

Since the focus of this book is on finding the major points of intuition, we will assume that interest rates and dividend yields are zero. There is not much additional widely applicable insight to be gleaned by varying those parameters.

We will assume an underlying current spot price of 100 because most options are eventually priced and quoted as a percentage of the underlying spot price anyway, and because strikes are usually normalized in the same way as well.

## Simulation

For concreteness we will usually assume a one-year maturity with daily time steps. That means there will be 252 simulated daily returns. Why 252? That is a magic number in finance because it is the assumed number of business days per year in American markets, calculated as 365 calendar days minus 52 times 2 weekend days minus 9 holidays. Daily average returns are annualized by multiplying by 252; daily return standard deviations are annualized by multiplying by the square root of 252; one-year simulations of daily returns involve simulating 252 time steps; variance swap terms often specify a multiplier of 252 in the term sheets. It is a magic number.

The most important parameter for our Black-Scholes simulation is the volatility. Let's start by assuming the volatility is 20 percent. It's a nice round number and it is relatively close to the historical average of many securities.

To start, let's assume an at-the-money option. Our task is now to simulate a single path of 252 daily returns, calculate the Black-Scholes delta on the option for each day and hedge it, compute the total profit or loss from such hedging, and compare it to the expected profit or loss. We hope to see a number very near zero for the total, which would validate the Black-Scholes model. Remember that it doesn't matter which random path we take because Black-Scholes is supposed to hold perfectly across every single possible path.

### 5.2.1 *A simple approximation*

Let's begin with the simplest question. We are buying a one-year at-the-money call option on an underlying security with 20 percent annualized volatility and no dividends in an environment with zero interest rates. What is the Black-Scholes model price of such an option?

There is a simple and useful rule of thumb for evaluating at-the-money options. The model price, expressed as a portion of the underlying spot price, will be:

$$0.4\sigma\sqrt{T}$$

Technically, this approximation only applies to options whose strike price equals the fair forward price of the underlying security. These are often called "at-the-money-forward" or "ATMF" options. One nice feature of European ATMF options is that calls and puts have the exact same price, so the approximation works whether you are evaluating an ATMF put or call. (This follows from the put-call parity discussed in Chapter 4: when the strike of a forward is the fair forward strike, the value of the forward is by definition zero, so the difference between the call and put prices with that strike is zero. See Equation (4.1).)

This approximation is easy to remember because all you have to recall is that the price is proportional to the *total volatility*. The total volatility is the unannualized amount of volatility expected on the underlying security. If you expect annual volatility of $\sigma$, then over the entire life of the option, namely the maturity $T$, you would expect the total volatility to be $\sigma\sqrt{T}$, because volatility grows with the square root of time. And what is the constant of the proportionality? It is 0.4 — a little less than half.

In other words, to get access to all the gains from a stock over and above its fair forward price, you have to pay up front a little less than half of its one-sigma move. Sounds like a pretty fair deal, no?

If you imagine that the stock return is approximately normal, then your at-the-money option has a fifty percent chance of ending up in the money. What is the probability that it ends up so far in the money that you actually make a net profit?

We can compute this as the area under the normal distribution from 0.4 to infinity, or equivalently because the normal distribution is symmetric, from negative infinity to -0.4. This probability is 34.46 percent. Taken all together, this means you have about a one-in-three chance of making a net profit on an at-the-money option for which you paid the Black-Scholes price, about a one-in-two chance of losing your entire premium, and the remainder (about a one-in-six chance) of losing only a part of what you paid.

Given that when you do end up in-the-money you can possibly get very high returns, these seem to be reasonable probabilities. If nothing else, they are at least intuitively easy to remember. So the formula for the approximation of 0.4 times the total volatility can come quickly to your mind.

So, for our one-year ATM option (which is also technically ATMF because interest rates and dividends are zero), the approximately correct price, expressed as a portion of the underlying spot price, is:

$$0.4 \cdot 0.2 \cdot \sqrt{1} = 0.08 = 8\%$$

The actual price using the exact Black-Scholes pricing formula is 7.96557 percent of the spot price. It is a very good approximation.

### 5.2.2 Puzzles and bugs

The question is, if we paid out $8 to buy the option, will the dynamic delta hedging strategy over the next twelve months result in exactly $8 of profit?

After all, the Black-Scholes model insists that the net profit or loss (or "P&L") will be zero for any option purchased at the fair Black-Scholes price on an underlying following Black-Scholes dynamics, no matter what the actual path is in the future of the underlying.

> "Beware of bugs in the above code; I have only proved it correct, not tried it."
>
> *Donald E. Knuth*

Let's first consider two easier warm-up puzzles. The first is this: if we believe the Black-Scholes model, and the model says that we will make up our $8 initial cash outlay simply by following their dynamic trading strategy, why not just do the dynamic trading strategy and save ourselves the $8 we would have paid for the option? If the model says we would have a net zero P&L when including the $8 loss on the option premium, then if we just do the delta hedging, we should simply make $8. No loss.

What's the bug in this reasoning?

You might say that without the option you don't know what the right delta is, that is, how many shares you should buy or sell each day for the dynamic delta hedging strategy.

But that objection can be overcome. We could just imagine that we bought a particular option, and calculate the delta we would have had, if we had bought it. And then just hedge to it.

You might say that we can't be sure it will work every time, because we don't have the option position. True, but even if we only expect to make $8 on average, with some noise around it, that is still a great trade.

So why not do it?

Before answering, let's pose the second easy puzzle: how should you respond to someone who claims to have discovered a better dynamic trading strategy for hedging options in a Black-Scholes world? Imagine this person bursts into your morning research meeting and says that hedging every other day instead of every day, or only following upticks, or some other crazy filter, results in a positive net P&L rather than a zero net P&L as per Black-Scholes, even in a Black-Scholes world. Should you hire this person immediately? Or call security?

> "He wasn't Bugs without the gags we gave him."
>
> *Tex Avery*, about Bugs Bunny

The bug in the first question is the same as the bug in the second question, and it is a common mistake made even by top practitioners: the drift term of the underlying only disappears when your net delta is zero. In other words, an unhedged option cannot be priced with no-arbitrage methods.

More specifically, if you only do the dynamic delta hedging, but you are not actually hedging anything, then you are not delta-neutral each day, but are instead constantly taking directional market risk. The size of your bet changes as your imagined option delta changes.

So the first claim is equivalent to announcing that you have found some kind of timing strategy to just trade shares of the underlying security, with no options involved. But we have assumed that the underlying security returns are distributed randomly. You can't consistently make money just by buying and selling shares when prices move about randomly. So the first claim cannot hold, and it's easy to imagine a counterexample: a deep-in-the-money call option will have a delta near one, so your trading strategy would be to sell the market, with not much rebalancing after that. But if the market just keeps going up after that, you will just keep losing money.

The resolution of the second puzzle is the same. If there were a better way to hedge than simply neutralizing the delta as often as possible, then you could construct a pure stock trading strategy on a random underlying that would still make money. Here's how: take a long position in an option and hedge it with the new method, take a short position in the same option and hedge that with the standard Black-Scholes method. Then your net position every day has zero options and some amount of stock equal to the excess of the new method over the Black-Scholes method. At best, this excess position is zero; most of the time, it is some arbitrary position in the market. And again, as we have assumed that the underlying follows the random fluctuations of the Black-Scholes model, there can't be any stock-only trades that consistently make money.

With that intuition in mind, we are now ready to test Black-Scholes.

### 5.2.3 Random numbers

In matters of law and justice, there are two kinds of questions: questions of fact and questions of law.

Questions of fact are things like, how fast was the car moving, what jacket was the defendant wearing, what time of day was it.

Questions of law are things like, murder requires an intentional act, contracts are void when there is no meeting of the minds, jointly held property accrues to the remaining party when one dies, etc.

Similarly with financial engineering, there are questions of fact and questions of models.

Questions of fact are things like, does the underlying distribution have excess kurtosis relative to a normal distribution, are the returns autocorrelated, what is the best estimate of future volatility.

Questions of models are things like, what happens if we hedge every other day instead of every day, how does the sensitivity to model parameters change as the underlying changes, etc.

In questions of law, the facts are assumed to be known, and often interpreted in the most favorable possible light to the potential loser in the action. For example, if you make a motion for a summary judgment, the judge will interpret the facts in the light most favorable to your opponent, and render a legal decision. That means that even if we accept your opponent's story, he would still lose, as a matter of law.

Similarly, in questions of models, the facts are assumed to be known, and interpreted in the most favorable possible light to the model. So if we want to see if a model is consistent, we will assume all of the facts are exactly as the model wishes them to be. In the case of Black-Scholes, that means we assume that returns are as continuous as possible and are generated by a lognormal process. For simplicity, we can also assume that interest rates and dividend yields are zero.

So let's test the model by seeing if our hedging P&L really does offset the model cost of the option, along every single possible path.

We have bought a one-year ATM call for $7.97. The underlying is $100 and returns are lognormally distributed with 20% annualized volatility. What would be the return on the underlying on the first day?

(a) Zero.
(b) A random number between zero and one.
(c) Whatever the daily riskfree rate is.

The answer is none of the above.

The first day's return is the change in price from today until tomorrow, so it is not necessarily zero, and it is a random number, but not necessarily between zero and one.

It would be a random number drawn from the appropriate lognormal distribution, not the uniform distribution.

Getting a uniformly random real number between zero and one is easy. Virtually every programming language has some way to do that. In Microsoft Excel, you can type the following formula into any cell:

=RAND()

How can we get a random number drawn from a lognormal distribution, or any other distribution other than the uniform?

We can use the following trick. Think of the cumulative distribution function of any distribution, for example, the lognormal distribution.

It looks something like this:

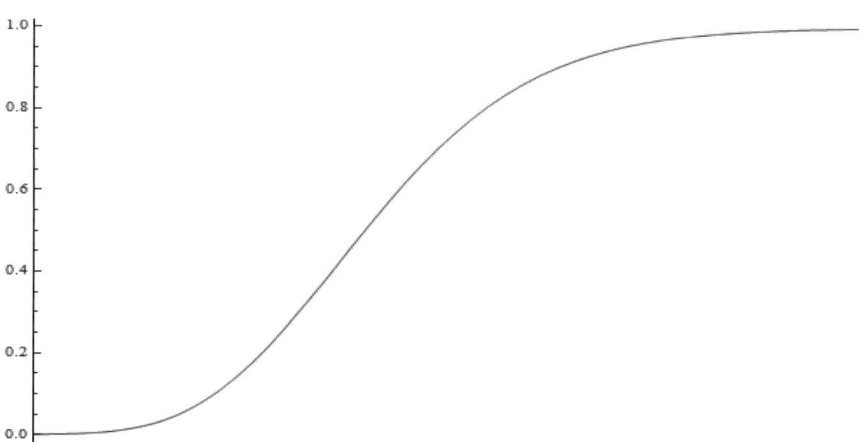

Figure 5.1. The CDF of the lognormal distribution

The cumulative probability starts at zero and grows up to one. What we want to get is a random number along the *x*-axis. But notice two things: the *y*-axis is always between zero and one, and for every *y* value, there is a unique corresponding *x* value. The trick is then to pick a uniformly random number between zero and one as the cumulative probability, and then find the matching *x* value that generates that probability. In Excel 2010, the formula would look like this:

$$=\text{LOGNORM.INV(RAND(),0,0.2)}$$

It works by taking the inverse of the lognormal CDF relative to a random cumulative probability, given the assumed parameters of the lognormal distribution. In this example, we assumed $\mu = 0$ and $\sigma = 0.2$.

Running that example generates random numbers like this: 1.02936, 0.798923, 0.812552, etc. What do these numbers represent?

(a) These numbers represent the ratio $S_1/S_0$, meaning tomorrow's price divided by today's price.
(b) These numbers represent the return $S_1/S_0 - 1$.
(c) These numbers represent the logreturns $\ln(S_1/S_0)$.

The most correct answer is (a). The price tomorrow will be $100 times 1.02936 (or 0.798923 or 0.812552 etc.). But it's not necessarily *tomorrow* per se. What is the actual time horizon for which we simulated a logreturn?

(a) One day.
(b) One week.
(c) One month.
(d) One year.

The answer is (d), one year. How can you tell? The easiest way is to look at the second parameter of the lognormal distribution, where we have input $\sigma = 0.20$. This is an annualized number, and so we are drawing numbers that are distributed with a one-year volatility of 20%. To simulate a daily return, we need to scale the volatility down to a single day. The Excel 2010 code for this is:

```
=LOGNORM.INV(RAND(),0,0.2/SQRT(252))
```

Now, let's make sure it is correct. If we simulate 252 such numbers, and take the product, we should have simulated one single yearly number. In other words, if we line up 252 columns in a row with the code above, and then multiply them all through, and we do that on 1,000 consecutive rows, then we will have simulated 1,000 paths, and on each path, we will have calculated its terminal stock price.

What should the average of those terminal stock prices be? It should be 100, right? Because we simulate with zero drift and some fixed volatility?

Wrong.

Why is it wrong? Why should the average not be 100?

This is a very confusing point to some people and a very obvious one to others. To those who find it confusing, there are two ways of looking at it: a mathematical way and an empirical way.

The mathematical way is this: what is the expected value of a random variable following a lognormal distribution derived from a normal distribution with mean $\mu$ and standard deviation $\sigma$? One could evaluate the integral or one could rely on symbolic manipulation languages like Mathematica.

In Mathematica, one need only write the following:

```
Expectation[x, x≈LogNormalDistribution[μ,σ]]
```

This brief code computes the expectation of a random variable $x$ following the given distribution. Mathematica immediately gives the answer:

$$e^{\mu+\sigma^2/2}$$

In other words, even when there is no drift, so that $\mu = 0$, the expected value of the lognormal distribution is affected by the volatility.

Thus, to simulate paths with truly zero drift, we have to subtract $\sigma^2/2$ from the drift. That's the mathematical approach.

The empirical approach is to just take those 1,000 paths we simulated and compute the average. Or note that we do not actually need to simulate and then aggregate up the daily returns, but we can simulate yearly returns directly. Further, we can do it many times, and we don't need to do it in Excel, where adding thousands of rows can be a bit cumbersome at times. In Mathematica, we can write:

```
Mean[RandomVariate[
    LogNormalDistribution[0, .2],
    10000000]]
```

and within seconds see that the average over 10 million paths is 1.0201.

So now we have learned something many people overlook or forget: when you are simulating lognormal returns, you always have to subtract away half the variance from the drift. This is far and away the most common mistake in simulating returns.

### 5.2.4 The Black-Scholes macros and functions

If you are in the derivatives world, you will use the Black-Scholes functions early and often, in whatever operating system and programming language you use. You may decide to build them yourself; in fact, doing so may be one of your first assignments if you are new on the desk. And if it is your assignment, then by all means you should do it. It will likely be used as a test of your programming ability and financial competence.

But once you have risen past that entry level test, you will never code the functions yourself. Doing so would be a waste of time. A financial hacker would not hesitate to search the web for free or cheap libraries.

Once you find them, you will need the following functions:

- BSCallPrice and BSPutPrice, to calculate the Black-Scholes price of a European call or put respectively.
- BSCallDelta, BSCallGamma, BSCallVega, and BSCallTheta, and similar ones for puts. Note that the gamma and vega of a call is always the same as that of a put with the same strike and maturity on the same underlying.
- BSCallImpliedVolatility and BSPutImpliedVolatility to back out the volatility implied by a given market price.

Of course, the particular package you choose may have slightly different names for these functions. It may, for example, simply have functions called Price, Delta, etc., where one of the parameters defines whether to evaluate it as a call or as a put. Ultimately, however, you will have functions similar to those listed above.

The parameters to such functions will include the following:

- Information about the option: the type of the option whether a call or a put, the strike price $X$, and the time to expiry in years $T$.
- Information about the underlying: the current price $S$, the annualized volatility $\sigma$, and the dividend yield $q$ (if any).
- Information about the world: the risk-free rate $r$.

For concreteness, let's suppose that the functions are named based on the type of the option (call or put) and that the rest of the parameters are passed in the same order as listed above: $X, T, S, \sigma, q, r$.

Of course, your particular functions may differ in name or in the order of the parameters, but the adjustment is trivial. The benefit of the canonical ordering of the parameters as above is that it is easy to remember: they go from most specific to most general, starting from a description of the particular option and ending with a description of the world.

## 5.2.5  A few days to start, and an error

Let us simulate just a handful of days, to start. Note that this section 5.2.5 contains exactly one error. The next section 5.2.6 will discuss what it is.

It's easiest to start in Excel. Each row will be a day, and we'll have five rows to represent five days. Today is the first row, and the first day, and the expiration will be on the fifth row, the fifth day. There are four (business) days from now until then so we are looking at an option with expiry $T = 4/252$.

The columns are the information we need for each day. They are:

(1) The current remaining expiry on the option. On day one, it is $4/252$. On day two, it is $3/252$, and so on. On day five, it is $0/252$; the option has expired.
(2) The current underlying price. On day one, it is assumed to be $100$. On day two, it will be the day one price times a random lognormally distributed number.
(3) The current delta of the option. This will always be computed by the BSCallDelta function applied to the strike $X$, the current remaining expiry from column 1, the current underlying price from column 2, the volatility $\sigma$, the dividend yield $q$, and the risk-free rate $r$. The only inputs that change each day are the remaining expiry and the underlying price.
(4) The hedging P&L (profit or loss) for that day. This is the most important column.

The hedging P&L is supposed to reflect how much money we made or lost in our stock trades, trades that we instituted to hedge the delta from our option. How do we calculate it?

We could memorize a formula, but it is all too easy to use the wrong rows or in the wrong order or insert or delete a negative sign. Let's reason it out.

First, ask yourself, *what time* is represented on each row? Sure, we know that row 1 is day 1, but *what time* on day 1? Is it noon? The opening bell? The close? We need the information both to compute our exposure and then to trade, so we need to be careful not to accidentally use information from the future to determine trades today.

The easiest way of thinking about it is to assume that each row represents the close, or, if it helps, a microsecond before the close. Think of yourself as a trader charged with hedging this option. Just before the close, you re-evaluate your position. Another day has passed, so your expiry has declined by one day. And the underlying price has moved. So you can calculate what your new delta is.

Given this new delta, you have to go into the market immediately and hedge yourself. So if the new delta on your option position is, for example, 200 shares, then what do you need to do in the market?

(a) Sell 200 shares.
(b) Buy 200 shares.

The answer is sell 200 shares. Your delta is +200 shares, meaning your exposure is long 200 shares. If you forget to hedge and the market goes up, you are lucky and happy. If it goes down, you are fired. So you need to put on a trade that will let you sleep at night. That means offsetting your exposure, so you need to sell 200 shares.

What will be the profit or loss from your sale of 200 shares? As of today, you do not know. It depends on where you buy back those shares, and, of course, where you sold them today.

Let's assume that you can always trade at the closing price, the same price you used in your input to calculate your delta. This is a reasonable assumption because calculating delta can be done very fast. Even in situations where the derivative is far too complicated for the simple

Black-Scholes formula or even some combinations of them, even if it can take hours to calculate the price of the derivative in a new scenario, you can calculate the delta for a wide variety of possible closing prices ahead of time, and then just look up the value in a table. If the derivative is not overly sensitive to particular values, you can even interpolate between values, making it even easier.

Further, the amount you hedge is usually not an enormous percentage of daily volume, and so your hedging amount should not cause too much market impact. Of course, this is not always the case, but for our purposes of validating Black-Scholes, we assume its assumptions hold, including the assumption of no transactions costs, market impact, slippage, or commissions.

Thus, your profit tomorrow from your hedging trades today would be equal to the amount of shares you traded multiplied by the change in the underlying price. So if you sold 200 shares and the underlying price fell from $99.50 to $99.25, your hedging P&L would be $50.

On which row should you account for this hedging P&L? Should it be on the row and the date when you put on the trade, or when you took it off? Specifically, should it be on the row when the underlying is at $99.50, or at $99.25?

This question does not have a necessarily wrong answer. Mathematically, you could put it in either row, as long as you were careful about the last row.

But philosophically, the P&L should be entered on the row when it is known. We do not know the P&L ahead of time. The big picture to remember here is to never let any value in any row depend on anything from later rows.

This is a common and subtle and frustrating mistake, especially when developing trading strategies. It is surprisingly easy to accidentally have your strategy today depend on data from tomorrow. Even if there is noise in how it depends on it, you will end up with great looking performance, and you can spend a long time tracking down the bug. The best thing to do in such a situation is enjoy the feeling of omnipotence temporarily and bask in the glory of a seemingly infallible strategy. Once that feeling subsides, then you can more calmly look for the error. And if you don't find an error, then maybe you have found a great strategy!

So what number goes in the hedging P&L column for the first day?

(a) The option delta from day one times the increase in the underlying price from day one to day two.
(b) Nothing; the option delta times the increase in price should go into the hedging P&L column for the second day.

The answer is none of the above. It is true that nothing should go into the hedging P&L for day one, because there has not been any profit or loss to speak of. In reality, the hedging P&L for that day would simply be the slippage between where you actually executed your hedge and the closing price, but here we are assuming no slippage.

But it should not go into the second row either because the formula is not quite correct. It is missing a negative sign. Remember, the option delta is the exposure you have if you do not trade; the hedge you need to do is the opposite of your option delta.

Here is what the Excel formulas would look like for the first row of data (it is a good idea to keep the first few rows blank to leave room for summary statistics or other calculations):

| Cell | Title | Formula |
|------|-------|---------|
| A4 | Expiry | =4/252 |
| B4 | Stock | 100 |
| C4 | Delta | =BSCallDelta(100,A4,B4,.2,0,0) |
| D4 | Hedge P&L | |

And here is what the Excel formulas would look like for the next row:

| Cell | Title | Formula |
|------|-------|---------|
| A5 | Expiry | =A4-1/252 |
| B5 | Stock | =B4*LOGNORM.INV(RAND(), 0-1/2*(0.2*SQRT(1/252))^2, 0.2*SQRT(1/252)) |
| C5 | Delta | =BSCallDelta(100,A5,B5,.2,0,0) |
| D5 | Hedge P&L | =-C4*(B5-B4) |

The new expiry merely decrements by one business day.

The new stock price is the old stock price multiplied by a random number drawn from a lognormal distribution with an associated drift of zero (adjusted for the volatility as described in Section 5.2.3) and a standard deviation of $\sigma/\sqrt{T} = 0.2/\sqrt{252}$.

The new delta is the same formula as the old delta, but using the new expiry and underlying price.

The hedging P&L calculates the amount of money you made or lost from yesterday's trade.

The formulas for the remaining rows are exactly the same, including the last row. This is an additional benefit of never using information from the future. If we had associated the hedging P&L with the date of entry into the trade, we would have had to be careful to be sure that the last row was blank, otherwise we would accidentally calculate the profit assuming we liquidated our delta hedge tomorrow at a blank price, or zero.

You might wonder why we don't need to keep track of all of our stock trades. After all, if we sold 200 shares on day one, and then our option delta turned out to be 250 on day two, we only need to sell an additional 50 shares, and so it seems we need to compute the P&L from each of our trades individually.

> "I can't be expected to keep track of all my wheelings and dealings!"
>
> *Homer Simpson*

Here's the assumption hidden in our formula: it is true in that example that you only need to sell an additional 50 shares, but, equivalently, you can imagine that you bought back all 200 shares that you sold the day before, and then sold again 250 shares. This way, you can calculate the hedging P&L based only on your net stock position each day, and not have to keep track of each individual trade.

You would, however, have to keep track of each individual trade once you take transactions costs into account, because you would not want to pay commissions to both buy and sell 200 shares with yourself for no economic benefit.

Okay, so now that this is done, we can test Black-Scholes. Remember that according to Black-Scholes, the total profit from hedging should exactly offset the initial cost of the option. In our example, a five-day option on a 20-vol stock should cost $1, a number we can compute either from the Black-Scholes formula or from the approximation in Section 5.2.1:

$$\$100 * 0.4 * 0.2 * \sqrt{4/252} = \$1$$

But what is the total hedging P&L? Because we have assumed the interest rate is zero, we can just sum up the daily hedging P&L's. (If the interest rate were not zero, we would have to adjust them all to compare it with the initial premium on the same day.)

If you run this spreadsheet, each time you recalculate (using F9 as a shortcut), you get different results because of the different random numbers. Sometimes the hedging P&L comes out to about $1. This is good, because it cost you $1 to buy the option, and you made $1 hedging, so your net profit is zero, exactly as Black-Scholes predicts.

But sometimes, the hedging P&L is more than $1, so you actually make some net money. That's okay as far as it goes, but what if you had sold the option? Then you would have lost money, and that's not so good. But this is only a minor problem.

The major problem is that much of the time, you end up losing money on your hedging P&L. Not just failing to make up the entire $1 you spent on the option, but actually losing money. Losing an extra $0.20, or $1, or even $3.

That is unacceptable. We have simulated a Black-Scholes world and hedged exactly as Black-Scholes requires, and yet we have lost money. The hedge was supposed to offset the cost of our option, but we would have been better off not hedging at all. At least then we would have limited our losses to just the initial premium. But because we hedged exactly as we were supposed to, we lost even more money? Thanks a lot, Black-Scholes!

Is this a bug in Black-Scholes?

Maybe Black-Scholes doesn't work exactly on each path after all. Maybe it is only true on average.

Did people not know about this problem?

Is this why the financial system collapsed in the late 2000's?

Is this why Long-Term Capital Management, the hedge fund that once boasted Nobel laureates and derivatives pioneers Myron Scholes and Robert Merton as partners, lost more than 90 percent of its assets in 1998?

Is this a fatal error in the foundation of finance?

## 5.2.6 Fixing the error

The error is not in Black-Scholes. Perhaps this makes you feel relief and hope in the stability of our financial system. It shouldn't. On the contrary, if you believed that our financial system depended on a model being right, then you should be panicking. No model is right.

What you should feel is terror, a cold sweat on your neck, because the error in the previous section is another common mistake. It is easy enough to spot in such a simple scenario (have you spotted it yet?), but when the going gets tough and the derivatives become more complicated, such a mistake can slip past many an otherwise careful trader and programmer.

The error is this: the total P&L is not just the difference between the hedging P&L and the initial option premium. There is a missing piece. The general lesson here is in how to make sure you don't miss any sources of P&L.

To do that, always carefully list all of your trades, and make sure you have calculated the market price of each of them at the end.

In this case, the stock trades are well accounted for. Every trade has been marked.

But you had another position. You had a position in options. You bought the call option on day one for $1. What was it worth on day five, at expiry?

About half the time, it is worthless, because the stock price ended below the strike of $100.

But the other half of the time, it was worth its intrinsic value, or the excess of the underlying price over $100. We did not account for that.

The total P&L is thus, in generality, the hedging P&L, minus the initial option premium, plus the terminal option intrinsic value. Alternatively and equivalently, it is the hedging P&L plus the option

P&L, where the option P&L is the change in price of the option from when you bought it to when it expired.

If we look at this revised total P&L in the spreadsheet of five days, we no longer see large losses of $4. But the total P&L is not always exactly zero either. It can be zero or negligible such as $0.01 for certain paths, and we would think a few pennies here or there are no big deal. But we also occasionally still see total P&L ranging from a $1 loss to a more than $1 gain.

Given that the option value itself is only about $1, this represents a return of between -100% and +100% over just one week, when the Black-Scholes model allegedly predicts exactly 0% return.

What is going on?

The answer to this puzzle is in the next chapter.

# Chapter 6

# Puzzles and Bugs

There are a lot of common mistakes, or bugs, made when developing or testing advanced derivative valuation models, and many of those same bugs crop up even when the model is plain old Black-Scholes. Many highly experienced derivatives traders and researchers will miss at least one of the puzzles and bugs in this chapter. If you understand them here, then you will immunize yourself to them in more complicated situations, and be a step ahead of the competition.

## 6.1 Why Did We Lose All That Money?

What do we do when things go wrong? Many traders facing mounting losses are often relegated to the pit of despair known as "P&L decomp."

P&L decomp is short for profit and loss decomposition, the process of explaining why certain positions made or lost money.

It asks questions like: "How much should we have made from hedging? How much did we actually make? And how much should we have made from changes in parameters? How much did we actually make?"

> "Lucy, you got some 'splainin' to do!"
> *Ricky Ricardo*, "I Love Lucy" (1951)

At the end, after asking all possible reasonable questions, whatever is left over, if anything, is called the *residual* P&L. This number ought to be near zero, otherwise you haven't decomposed enough.

Another way of thinking about it is that you start with your residual P&L equal to your true P&L, the amount of money you actually made or lost, and then you split it up into buckets for better understanding, until hopefully your residual bucket is quite small.

But we can't even begin to properly do P&L decomp until we understand the "Greeks," the various mathematical derivatives of financial derivatives.

> "I fear the Greeks, even when they bring gifts."
>
> *Virgil*

Suppose you own a call option with a delta of 0.4, but you made a mistake hedging. Instead of selling 0.4 shares, you actually bought 0.4 shares. So your net delta, which should be zero if you are hedging correctly, is instead long 0.8 shares of the underlying. This is a big blunder.

How much money will you lose tomorrow?

(a) You will lose 0.8 times the percentage change in the underlying.
(b) You will lose 0.8 times the dollar change in the underlying.
(c) You will lose 0.8 in the notional units of the underlying, e.g. $0.80 if the underlying is denominated in dollars.

The answer is none of the above. If the underlying price goes up, you are net long delta, so you will actually make a profit, not a loss.

"Okay," you sigh, "then let's suppose the underlying falls tomorrow. Then what is the correct answer?"

The correct answer is still none of the above. However, of the choices given, (b) is the closest because delta by definition is the change in the derivative for a unit change in the underlying price:

$$\Delta = \partial V / \partial S \tag{6.1}$$

But (b) is not the whole story. This is not your total P&L; it is only the delta P&L, or the P&L that is due to the initial net delta having been different from zero:

$$\text{Delta P\&L} = \Delta(S_1 - S_0) \tag{6.2}$$

Your total profit or loss will *not* exactly equal your net delta times the change in the underlying price.

Why not?

For one reason: because your net delta will change right along with changes in the underlying price.

Remember gamma? Gamma is the change in delta for a unit change in the underlying price:

$$\Gamma = \partial \Delta / \partial S = \partial^2 V / \partial S^2 \tag{6.3}$$

At the end of the day tomorrow, if the price has dropped from $S_0$ to $S_1$, then your delta will have dropped from $\Delta$ down to $\Delta + \Gamma(S_1 - S_0)$.

So, what would your profit or loss tomorrow be?

(a) Your initial net delta times the change in the underlying.
(b) Your final net delta times the change in the underlying.
(c) The average of (a) and (b).

Again, the correct answer is none of the above, because your gamma would change too. In principle, we could keep going to higher and higher orders of partial derivatives, and for big moves, those higher order terms may be important. But in most cases, they are not.

So ignoring the higher order terms, the closest correct answer would be (c). In other words, the change in the underlying price times your initial net delta increased by half the change in the delta due to gamma. But bear in mind that the change in delta depends on the change in the underlying itself. That's why the gamma P&L, or the portion of your total P&L that is due to the delta changing because of gamma, depends on the square of the change in the underlying price:

$$\text{Gamma P\&L} = \frac{1}{2}\Gamma(S_1 - S_0)^2 \tag{6.4}$$

Another way to see that is to write the sum of delta P&L and gamma P&L together:

$$\text{Delta P\&L} + \text{Gamma P\&L} = \left(\Delta + \frac{1}{2}\Gamma(S_1 - S_0)\right)(S_1 - S_0)$$

But it would still be the wrong answer to the question of *total* P&L, even if there are no higher order terms than gamma.

Why?

Because time passed.

The valuation of every option is subject to time. As time passes, options usually lose money because they have a shorter expiry. This sensitivity to time is called theta:

$$\Theta = \partial V / \partial t \tag{6.5}$$

And the portion of your total P&L that is explained by theta is your theta P&L:

$$\text{Theta P\&L} = \Theta(t_1 - t_0) \tag{6.6}$$

Assuming that nothing else changes, i.e., the implied volatility, interest rate, and dividends remain the same, then we can decompose your total P&L into the parts due to delta, gamma, and theta:

Total P&L = Delta P&L + Gamma P&L + Theta P&L + Residual P&L

Notice the all-important residual P&L term at the end. That is where all the higher-order terms go to die. It includes the P&L due to such sensitivities as $\frac{\partial^2 V}{\partial s \partial t}$, $\frac{\partial^3 V}{\partial s^3}$, and so on.

The residual P&L term is the most critical one. That is the term you hope is close to zero, not too positive and not too negative. A lot of unexplained profits is almost as bad as a lot of unexplained losses because it suggests you are running an uncertain risk that you are not aware of.

> "I have known uncertainty: a state unknown to the Greeks."
>
> *Jorge Luis Borges*

## Puzzles and Bugs

This is a crucial point. The one overarching thing you want to do in finance is make money. But only slightly less important is to make it for the reasons you expected. Otherwise you may as well be gambling.

We have thus decomposed our total P&L into a delta P&L, a gamma P&L, and a residual P&L. We know that part of the residual P&L will be the higher order terms that we have ignored, but we think they will be usually quite small.

But, to answer all our earlier questions, what *is* our total P&L?

The total P&L is an accounting number. You just calculate how much money you would have today if you were able to liquidate all of your positions in an orderly manner, and subtract the similarly calculated number from yesterday. That's your total mark-to-market profit.

In other words, your total P&L is your market P&L, and the definitions and derivations above have served to do nothing more and nothing less than define the residual P&L as quite literally the remaining, unexplained P&L.

> "Your life is the sum of a remainder of an unbalanced equation inherent to the programming of the matrix. You are the eventuality of an anomaly, which despite my sincerest efforts I have been unable to eliminate from what is otherwise a harmony of mathematical precision. While it remains a burden assiduously avoided, it is not unexpected, and thus not beyond a measure of control."
>
> *The Architect*, "The Matrix Reloaded" (2003)

### 6.2 Should We Mark to Market or Model? To Mid or Bid?

In the introductory P&L decomposition above, we assumed that the total P&L was the market P&L, computed as the realized difference in the orderly liquidation value of your entire portfolio. But what is the orderly liquidation value of a derivative that is never sold?

It is an unobserved, and unobservable, number. It can be tested somewhat by liquidating a portion of your position. You could decide to sell and then buy back one percent of all of your positions every day.

Suppose it costs you $X$ to sell one percent of your positions and $Y$ to buy them back. You could then argue that the true value of your entire position is $100 \cdot (X + Y)/2$. This is typically called marking-to-mid, because you are marking the value of your portfolio to the mid-point of the market.

If you instead mark your position each day to $X$, then you are marking-to-bid.

Is marking-to-bid a more conservative measure of profit and loss than marking-to-mid?

(a) Yes, because you are using a more realistic measure of your liquidation value.
(b) No, because it is much easier to manipulate the bid price than the mid price.

The answer, as usual, is none of the above. Marking-to-mid is certainly more conservative on the first day, because your portfolio will be marked to a lower number.

But on each subsequent day, the difference may be higher, lower, or zero, depending on how the bid-offer spread changes with respect to changes in the underlying price.

As an example, consider a liquidity story. In this case, when the underlying price drops, liquidity dries up. When liquidity dries up, the bid-offer spread widens, because there are fewer people willing to provide tight markets.

In this case, marking-to-bid results in an even larger loss than marking-to-mid because the bid falls even more than the mid.

Conversely, in up markets, the bid-offer spread presumably tightens, so marking-to-bid results in an even larger profit than marking-to-mid because the bid rises even more than the mid.

Thus, it is not clear whether marking-to-bid is necessarily a better strategy than marking-to-mid.

> "When Greeks joined Greeks, then was the tug of war."
>
> *Nathaniel Lee*

Further, from the perspective of fairness, if occasionally new investors come in and old investors drop out, then marking-to-bid is a net benefit to new investors at the expense of old investors, because the new ones hold positions with relatively more expected return than if the positions had been marked-to-mid.

However, when they take their money out, they will also take it out at bid, so later investors may decide that it is approximately equivalent.

But the very first investors will get out at bid even though they entered, effectively, at mid, and were forced to bear the full cost of half of the bid-offer spread. There are lots of issues about fairness when it comes to marking to mid or to bid.

In doing P&L decomp, one approach might be to mark everything to liquidation value, and segregate out in one of the decomposition buckets the difference between the liquidation value and the mid-market value, and in another bucket the difference between the mid-market value and the model value.

Changes in the first would reflect changes in the underlying liquidity or the overall position held, while changes in the second would reflect changes in model cheapness or richness, and the remaining terms, being all model terms, would decompose the model changes into its own constituent parts.

## 6.3 Why Does the Hedged Profit Differ from Zero?

We saw in the previous chapter how a five-day Black-Scholes simulation of an at-the-money five-day call on a 20-vol non-dividend-paying stock in a world with zero interest rates could generate returns ranging from $-100\%$ to $+100\%$ when Black-Scholes asserts it should be zero always, along every path. How can that be?

Your first instinct might be that five days is just too coarse a time period. Black-Scholes assumes continuous movements and hedging, and daily is just not good enough, particularly when there are only five days until expiry, so that each interval carries enormous weight.

How can we test that instinct? Let's change the time intervals from days to hours. Instead of assuming we have five business days left with intervals of $dt = 1/252$, let's look at an option with just five hours left with intervals of $dt = 1/252/10 = 1/2520$. This implicitly assumes there are ten trading hours per day, which is acceptable as an approximation for now.

In that case, we can update our spreadsheet from the last chapter with the following formulas. Define some special cell to be $dt$. To do this, type = 1/2520 into your chosen cell, for example A1, and then click on the Name Box — the part of Excel to the left of the formula bar where it says "A1" — and change it to say "dt" instead. Then you can refer to it in formulas as "dt" directly, making them easier to read.

Here's what the formulas for the second row look like, with the remaining ones being essentially the same:

| Cell | Title | Formula |
|------|-------|---------|
| A5 | Expiry | =A4-dt |
| B5 | Stock | =B4*LOGNORM.INV(RAND(), 0-1/2*(0.2*SQRT(dt))^2, 0.2*SQRT(dt)) |
| C5 | Delta | =BSCallDelta(100,A5,B5,.2,0,0) |
| D5 | Hedge P&L | =-C4*(B5-B4) |

The total P&L is as before the sum of the total hedging P&L across all time periods and the change in the option price from the initial premium on hour one to its intrinsic value on hour five. The initial premium is about $0.32. What is the total P&L?

Sometimes it is near zero. But sometimes it is as low as -$0.30 and as high as +$0.30. In other words, it can still range from -100% return to +100% return. So your instinct does not seem to be validated. So let's go back to looking at daily instead of hourly changes.

But do not fret. Proving an instinct wrong is almost as valuable as proving it right. In some cases, it can be even more valuable, especially if it helps you to avoid mistakes in the future that you otherwise would have made.

> "Results! Why, man, I have gotten a lot of results. I know several thousand things that won't work."
>
> *Thomas Edison*

What is your next instinct? If the answer is not the size of the time difference in each interval, could it be the number of intervals? Maybe five of anything — be it hours or days — is just not enough to reduce the noise to the levels predicted by Black-Scholes.

A good financial hacker not only generates ideas but tests them too. Let's rerun our spreadsheet with 253 rows instead of 5. That would represent a year's worth of hedging on a daily basis, plus the initial day's values.

If Black-Scholes continues to fail in this scenario, and particularly if it continues to fail because the intervals are neither continuous enough nor plentiful enough, then Black-Scholes is not a useful model and we would have to explore other alternatives, because daily hedging is quite reasonable in the real world, particularly for a year-long option.

As a reminder, this exercise has ramifications far beyond Black-Scholes. Any valuation model on any more complicated derivative should still provide useful values even when hedging is not continuous.

To evaluate this possibility, we need to merely add more rows to our spreadsheet, change the initial maturity to be one year, and (this is a common Excel oversight) make sure we change our summation and other summary cells at the top to include the new, longer range of cells. Specifically, we need to make sure our intrinsic value refers to the last row, and the total hedging P&L sums across all of the rows, not just the first five.

Having done that, we can then try, as before, to recalculate numerous times to get a sense of how the total P&L changes. However, if we want to get a list of several hundred such total P&L across different paths, we need to copy the last three columns several hundred times and store the results somewhere.

This is where Excel can get cumbersome, and where it is useful to be able to rely on other tools. It is certainly possible to write Visual Basic code to run the simulation numerous times, and each time print the resulting total P&L to some special worksheet.

But using a higher level language such as Mathematica lets us automate and generalize a lot of the work.

For example, the very general code for simulating lognormal paths is:

```
Simulate[payoff_, n_:10000, μ_:0, σ_:.2, dt_:1/252, S0_:100, maturity_:1] :=
    payoff[FoldList[Times, S0, #]] & /@
        RandomReal[LogNormalDistribution[(μ - σ²/2) dt, σ Sqrt@dt],
            {n, Ceiling[maturity/dt]}]
```

The first line of the code above lists the input parameters and their default values. For those defaults, the third line generates 10,000 paths of 252 random daily returns. The second line computes the implied price paths from each of those 10,000 sequences of returns, and also applies an arbitrary function as the payoff to that sequence of prices. It uses the special "/@" shorthand notation for the Map function, to indicate a function being applied to each element of a list.

For example, if the payoff function were to simply return the last price in each path, then plotting the resulting histogram should show the terminal stock price distribution.

And indeed it does:

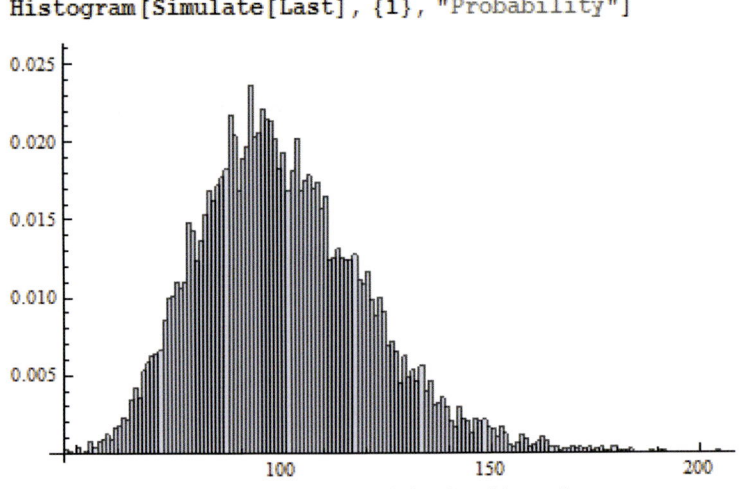

Figure 6.1. Histogram of simulated last price

We shall return to the general Simulate function later when we discuss exotic options. For now, let us explore what happens if we delta hedge each path.

All we need to do is define a payoff function that returns the total P&L from delta-hedging the option along that path according to the Black-Scholes delta at each point. We also want to express the total P&L as a portion of the initial option premium.

Here's the payoff function:

```
BSReturn[prices_, σ_ : .2, dt_ : 1 / 252, S0_ : 100, maturity_ : 1,
  strike_ : 100] :=
 (Max[Last[prices] - strike, 0] -
    MapIndexed[BSCallDelta[strike, maturity - (First@#2 - 1) dt,
        #, σ, 0, 0] &, Most@prices].Differences[prices]) /
   BSCall[strike, maturity, S0, σ, 0, 0] - 1
```

For the default parameters, and given a path of prices, the function calculates the intrinsic value and the initial option premium in the second and fourth lines above, and the total hedging P&L in the third line (and the first half of the fourth). The total hedging P&L is calculated as the dot product, meaning the total of the pairwise products, of the Black-Scholes call delta at each point in time and the subsequent change in underlying price.

It is not immediately obvious that we are multiplying by the subsequent difference in price rather than the preceding difference in price. This is a drawback of languages such as Mathematica and R. It is much easier to tell in Excel if you are using information from the future. That is why it is a good idea to first build some small test cases in Excel before automating it in a more formal language.

Here, we can eventually tell that we are using the subsequent price because the differences start with the second price minus the first price, and the deltas are calculated for each price starting with the first price. How do we know that it starts with the first price? Because we are looking at "Most@prices" and the Most function drops the last element, just as in Excel we never calculate the P&L from the last delta.

Another function we used in the definition of BSReturn was MapIndexed. This is similar to the Map function whose shorthand "/@" we used in the definition of Simulate, but which also passes the number of the element so that we can compute the remaining expiry.

The remaining expiry is calculated as the maturity minus the product of dt and what is effectively the current row number minus one. The current row number is accessed through MapIndexed as First@#2, meaning it is the first element of the second argument to the function that we are applying to the list. The slot "#" indicates the first argument, which is filled by the particular price at that point in the list.

You do not need to know or even understand Mathematica code. All of these examples could have been coded in R or Visual Basic or C or any other language. Indeed, it is a good exercise to try to code it in other languages. The presentation here is done with Mathematica for four reasons: because of its flexibility and generality, because of its numerous built-in functions that help leverage a financial hacker's time, because of its recent innovations in allowing interactive computations, and because its code is both relatively legible to someone unfamiliar with the language, and concise.

If we simulate 10,000 paths, what will the distribution of the total P&L be as a percentage of the initial option premium?

We hope that it is a percentage near zero, and indeed it seems to be an acceptable range:

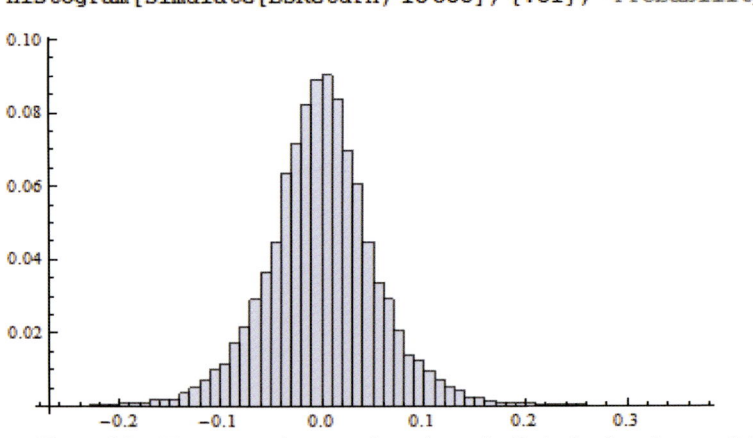

Figure 6.2. Histogram of returns from dynamically hedged option portfolio

The return from buying a one-year at-the-money call and hedging it daily using the Black-Scholes formula for the delta is zero percent return on average, with a range of about plus or minus 10 percent. The standard deviation of the return is 5 percent.

Why is it not exactly zero?

### 6.3.1 *How does the error depend on the hedging frequency?*

We can combine your two instincts and test what happens if we have 252*10 intervals of length $dt = 1/2520$; in other words, what happens as we hedge closer to continuously.

That histogram for 10,000 paths is shown in Figure 6.3.

```
Histogram[Simulate[BSReturn[#, .2, 1/2520] &,
    10000, 0, .2, 1/2520], {.0025}, "Probability"]
```

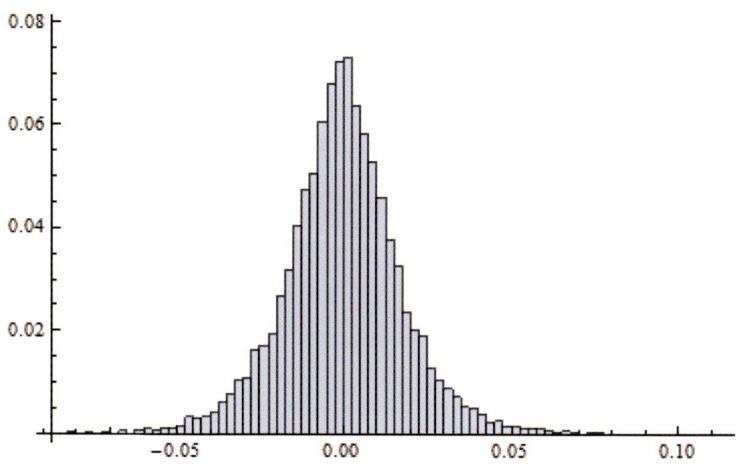

Figure 6.3. Histogram of returns from more frequently hedged option portfolio

The standard deviation of the hourly-hedging return is 1.8 percent, less than half of what it was for the daily-hedging return. Clearly the more frequently we hedge, the closer we get to the Black-Scholes prediction of zero P&L along every path. The noise around the zero percent comes from non-continuous hedging.

Though we are now hedging ten times as frequently, the standard deviation of our return due to the fact that it is still not continuous did not decline ten times but only by about two-thirds.

What is the relationship there? Is there a simple rule of thumb we can follow?

Figure 6.4 shows the standard deviation of returns for a few hedging frequencies ranging from once (daily) to one hundred (about every few minutes).

It looks like it declines proportionally to some inverse power of the hedging frequency. The best-fit curve shown that matches the data is the inverse square root.

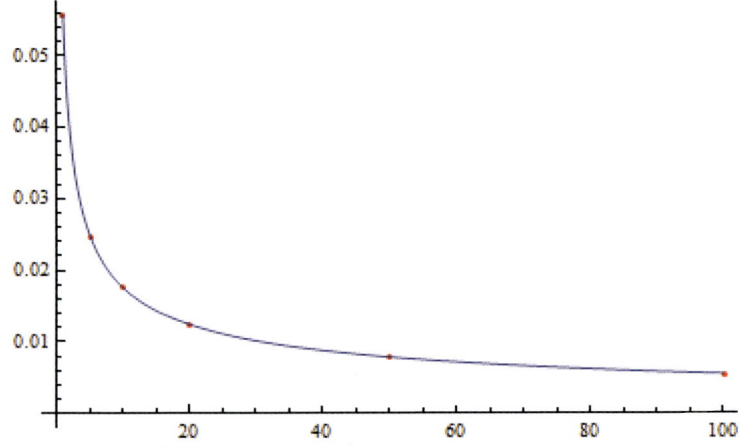

Figure 6.4. Standard deviation of returns to hedged portfolio vs. hedging frequency

Of course! That makes sense, doesn't it? We know volatility grows by the square root of time. So if we hedge ten times more frequently, each interval is one-tenth the size, and so the overall volatility should be the square root of one-tenth, which is about one-third.

We could have gotten that insight directly. If you did, that is great. But insight can be slippery, and failed insight can leave you right where you started. Hacking on the other hand is reliable, and even a failed attempt at financial hacking will have given you some progress to work from. For example, if you had guessed it declined like the reciprocal, or an exponential function, you would have quickly seen the fit is not very good, and you could have easily tweaked your code to test other variants.

In short, the inability to hedge perfectly continuously impacts your trading by introducing a random risk. That risk decreases if you hedge more frequently, but only as fast as a square root, so if you want to halve your risk, you have to hedge four times as often.

### 6.3.2 *Is the error too large?*

Is it too much? Is the five percent error from hedging daily too much of a risk? Do we need to throw away Black-Scholes because it is insufficiently useful as an approximation when hedging occurs daily rather than continuously? Is continuous time just a fun mathematical trick that has no bearing on reality?

How can we address this question? Five percent can sound like a lot or a little, depending on the context. What is the appropriate context?

In the land of options, the appropriate context is always volatility. What is the vega of a one-year at-the-money call option, or the sensitivity of the option price to a one point change in volatility?

We can calculate it as 0.397, or we can recall the approximation from Section 5.2.1 about the value of an at-the-money option, and take its derivative with respect to the volatility $\sigma$ to note that for $T = 1$, the vega should be about 0.4.

The vega is usually expressed in dollar terms. The price of the option, either calculated or using the approximation, is about \$8. So a one-point increase in volatility from 20% to 21% would raise the option price by $0.4/8 = 5\%$.

In other words, the noise from hedging a one-year option on a daily basis instead of continuously is about the same as one volatility point. So as a first test, we can ask if one vol point of noise renders Black-Scholes unusable. On first blush, it does not seem like too much noise; after all, when we estimate future volatility to be 20 percent, and it ultimately delivers 19 percent or 21 percent, we would not likely conclude that we were wrong. There is noise in realized volatility too.

As a first step, that's helpful, but it's not enough. We can also ask: is one volatility point too much extra risk?

Here's one way to think about it. Suppose this was the only risk in your options position. Would you still put on the trade?

To answer this question, you need to know how much money you expect to make on the option. Usually if you are making volatility bets and intend to hold the option to maturity, you'd like to make at least one vol point, maybe two or more. An exception might be if you are specifically in the high-volume, high-turnover business of making markets in options, and would try to get out earlier when possible.

If you are making one volatility point in expected profit, and the standard deviation of your profit is one volatility point, then your Sharpe ratio is about one. (The Sharpe ratio is the expected excess profit over the risk free rate divided by the standard deviation, but we are assuming the risk free rate is zero anyway.)

A Sharpe ratio of one is a pretty good trade. Not the best, not the worst. Pretty good. If the only risk from doing the option is the noise that comes from hedging daily rather than continuously, then this is likely a trade you will still want to do.

So in this second context, the noise is not too much to hinder a good trade. Therefore the Black-Scholes model is still useful.

A third way of looking at it is to compare it to transactions costs. The bid-offer spread of a one-year at-the-money call option is on the order of one volatility point in many markets; sometimes less. So the noise introduced into the model by hedging daily rather than continuously is on par with the market impact cost of trading the position. That doesn't seem to be too much either. So again, Black-Scholes is still useful.

Finally, the fourth way of looking at it is through the lens of diversification. The risk you are running here is market risk, but with the direction determined by the particular path followed by the underlying. If you have multiple options in different directions on the same underlying, your risk can be lessened, because the correlations among all those risks are less than one, and so diversification can make the portfolio of many options trades look better than each individually. Even more valuable would be to diversify your options book among different underlyings, particularly ones that are less correlated. Then your risk again diminishes.

So for these four reasons, we can conclude that yes, there is a risk to not hedging continuously, but even on a daily basis, it is not too large, it is comparable to the bid-offer spread or the expected profit, and it can be largely diversified away.

## 6.4 Should You Hedge to Model or Market?

You are working on an equity derivatives proprietary trading desk at a top international bank. One morning, a few minutes before a big research meeting with all the traders, the head of the desk tells you he wants you to talk for a few minutes at the meeting about whether options traders should hedge to model or to market. You nod okay but you're not really sure what he's talking about. Before you can ask any follow-up questions, the head of the desk has stepped out to get coffee. You know that when he comes back, it will be time for the meeting, and he will ask you to present to everybody. What do you do?

### 6.4.1 *The financial mathematician*

The financial mathematician would start deriving partial differential equations and imposing different boundary conditions.

He would attempt to first set everything up just right, make some simplifying assumptions, and combine complicated equations into a closed form solution, and then evaluate that closed form solution for the answers.

There is almost no way this can be done in a few minutes, and even if it somehow is done, it adds very little intuition relative to the long, detailed chain of mathematical work, where a single mistake in any of the links in the chain mean the entire result is wrong.

### 6.4.2 *The financial hacker*

But our approach as financial hackers is much more straightforward. First, we need to figure out what we are really talking about. What does it mean to hedge to model or market? How can you figure out what it means?

Always start with the basics. Let's say we bought a one-year at-the-money call option. What do the words "model" and "market" mean?

In general, with any option trade you put on and hedge to maturity, you must implicitly think the market price is incorrect. In this case, you bought the call because you thought it was cheap.

So your model price is _____ than the market price:

(a) higher
(b) lower

It must be higher. If your model price was lower than the market price, then that would mean you think the market is paying too much for the option, and you would sell it.

Okay, so the model price is what you think it ought to be worth and the market price is what the market says it is worth. Fine. But what does it mean to "hedge to" model versus market?

Recall what we did in the previous section in testing Black-Scholes. We bought an option, simulated the path of the underlying, and continually rebalanced our delta. That rebalancing of our delta was, of course, the hedging. In that example, we simulated stock returns having a 20 percent volatility, the implied volatility of our option was 20 percent, and the input to our delta calculation was also 20 percent. Which of those "20 percent" numbers is the hedging volatility?

The hedging volatility is:

(a) the implied volatility of the market price of the option on the day you buy it.
(b) the implied volatility of the model price of the option on the day you buy it.
(c) the recently realized historic volatility of the underlying.
(d) the volatility of the future simulated returns of the underlying.

The answer is none of the above. If you hedge assuming Black-Scholes, then the hedging volatility is the input to your call option delta formula. Recall that the delta of a call is a function like:

$$\Delta = \text{BSCallDelta}(K, T - t, S, \sigma, q, r) \tag{6.7}$$

where the fixed parameters $K$ and $T$ are the strike and maturity of the option, $S$ is the current underlying price, $t$ is the current time, $r$ is the interest rate, $q$ is the dividend yield, and $\sigma$ is the volatility.

That input $\sigma$ to the delta formula is your hedging volatility. You change that, and you change the volatility that you are hedging to.

So now the question is starting to take shape and make sense. If you hedge to model, then your $\sigma$ in the delta formula would be the model volatility that you predicted for the stock on day one. If you hedge to market, then your $\sigma$ in the delta formula would be the market implied volatility from day one.

For example, if we buy a call option at 20 vol, thinking it will realize 30 vol, should we hedge to 20 vol or 30 vol? And does the answer depend on whether the true vol is 20 or 30?

That's it! We've articulated an exact question. That is at least half the battle.

> "If I had an hour to solve a problem and my life depended on it, I would use the first 55 minutes to formulate the right question, because as soon as I have identified the right question, I can solve the problem in less than five minutes."
>
> *Albert Einstein*

Now, when you go to the morning meeting, you can say, "So here's my thinking on the question of hedging to model versus market. If we just look at a Black-Scholes world to start, what happens if we buy at 20 thinking it will be 30, and hedge to 20 versus 30, and see how our P&L looks, both when we are right and when we are wrong. And here are my results…"

Let's quickly get those results. Conceptually, we want the following columns in a spreadsheet for each point along a single path of the underlying (and then we will simulate thousands of paths):

(1) The time
(2) The stock price
(3) The delta of the option if we had hedged to 20 vol (model delta)
(4) The delta of the option if we had hedged to 30 vol (market delta)
(5) The hedging P&L on the model delta (yesterday's model delta times the change in stock price from yesterday to today)
(6) The hedging P&L on the market delta (calculated similarly)

Then, as before, the total P&L of the position would be the final intrinsic value of the option, minus the initial option price, plus the sum of the hedging P&L. We will assume zero interest rates and dividend yields to make things easier without losing any of the important intuition.

But how should we generate the stock prices? Should those simulations be done at 20 vol or at 30 vol?

The financial hacker doesn't think too long. There's no time. The financial hacker says, "Let's try both."

In fact, the financial hacker notices that there is no longer any concept of "model vol" or "market vol" in the simulations he's about to do. The key variables are rather the simulation vol which generates the stock prices and the hedging vol which determines the delta.

So really all we need to do is run all four combinations of simulation vol and hedging vol each being either 20% or 30% and see what the effect on the P&L is.

How can we easily measure the effect?

First, we can look at a histogram of the P&L, as we did in Section 6.3.

Second, we can look at how the total P&L is affected by the last price in the simulated stock price path.

And third, we can look at how the total P&L is affected by the realized volatility along the simulated stock price path.

The next page shows these three graphs for all four possibilities.

The relevant code is only a few simple lines:

```
modelVmarket[σhedge_, σsimul_, n_:1000, dt_:1./(252*4),
    S0_:100, K_:100, r_:0, q_:0, T_:1] :=
  Module[{initpx = BSCall[S0, K, r, q, σsimul, T],
    Ts = ReplacePart[Range[T, 0, -dt], -1 → ϵ]},
    Simulate[
      {Last@#, StandardDeviation@Differences@Log@# / Sqrt@dt,
        (BSCall[Last@#, K, r, q, σsimul, ϵ] - initpx -
          Dot[Most[BSCallDelta[#, K, r, q, σhedge, Ts]],
            Differences[#]]) / initpx} &, n, r - q, σsimul,
      dt, S0, T]];
```

### 6.4.3 *The histogram of the P&L*

There's a lot to learn from these graphs. Let's start with the P&L histogram when both the simulation and hedging volatilities are the same, either both 20% or both 30%. Then as before we see that the P&L is centered around zero and has a standard deviation of about 5 percent. It's nice to test new results by making sure they continue to agree with what we already know: it both verifies your code and provides context for the graphs to make it easier to spot the new differences.

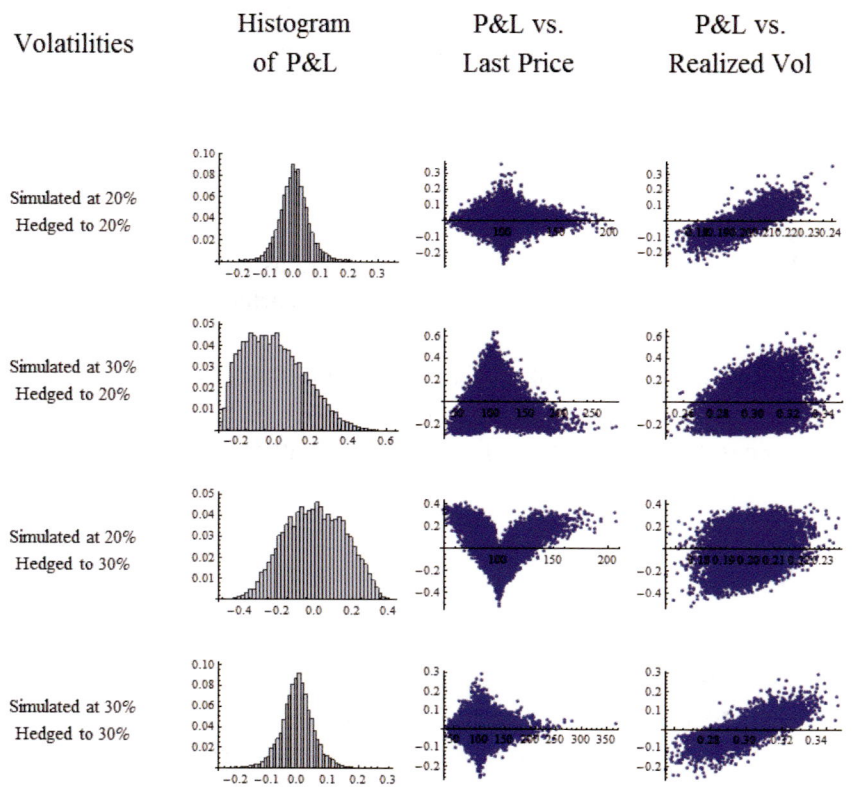

Figure 6.5. Market vs. model

Compare those P&L histograms when we hedge to the truth to those when we hedge away from the truth. When the underlying is drawn from a 30 vol distribution but we hedge to only a lower 20 vol, the standard deviation of the return is three times as high, at more than 15 percent. Even curiouser, the average is no longer centered around zero: the median return is negative. What is going on?

(The case when we hedge to the higher 30 vol on a 20 vol underlying is similar: the standard deviation is again 15 percent but the mean and the median are both positive. If we understand one, we would understand the other.)

### 6.4.4 *The scatterplot of the P&L versus the last price*

To make progress, we need to look at the second column of charts, plotting the P&L versus the last price in the underlying path. When we hedge to the truth at either 20 or 30 vol, the P&L is symmetric around the x-axis. This means that no matter where the stock price ends up at maturity, we are equally likely to have made money as to have lost money.

Why do the points taper off at the sides and bunch up and down in the middle? Imagine the extremes. If the stock ends up at a very low price, the delta of the call probably went to zero very quickly. There was therefore very little risk left. Once the delta became zero, there was no more hedging, and so it didn't matter whether you didn't hedge on a daily basis or you didn't hedge on a continuous basis.

Similarly, if the stock price ends up very high, then the delta of the call probably went to one very quickly. Again, there was therefore very little risk left. Once the delta became one, there was no more rebalancing of the hedge, and so it didn't matter whether you didn't rebalance on a daily basis or you didn't rebalance on a continuous basis.

But the plots in the cases where we didn't hedge to the truth is different. Let's focus now on the third row where we hedge to a higher vol than the truth. This is the prototypical case of hedging to the model. Presumably we believe the future realized volatility should be higher than the implied volatility of the price we bought it at. So we might consider hedging to our best forecast.

In that case when the hedge vol is 30 and the simulation vol is 20, the P&L as a function of the last price looks like a heart. It is not symmetric around the x-axis and it doesn't taper off at the sides: for terminal stock prices far from the initial stock price, we are guaranteed to have made a profit, and for terminal stock prices near the initial stock price, we are much more likely to have lost.

Why does it have this odd heart-shaped pattern?

(a) It is a mistake. We made an error somewhere.
(b) It is random. Run the simulations again and it will go away.

The answer is neither. The heart is real.

To figure out what is happening, again consider the extremes.

What does it mean if the stock ends up around 200? It probably means that the path was by and large straight up, because there is not enough time or volatility for the stock to have fallen first. The paths that end at the highest attainable levels of the underlying price must have attained those levels by going there as fast as possible, just like the winner in a sprint probably didn't dilly-dally along the way.

So if the underlying grew for much if not most of the history of the path, what kind of risk were you running by being mishedged?

Remember, you are hedging to a higher volatility than is being realized.

So is your delta along such a path higher or lower than it ought to have been?

(a) The model delta of the call, using 30 vol, was higher than the market delta of the call, using 20 vol, along the paths that ended up at high terminal values of the underlying price.
(b) No, the model delta was usually lower than the market delta.

To mix things up a little, the answer this time is not none of the above. It is just plain old (b).

To understand why on an intuitive level, recall that the delta can be thought of as approximately the probability of ending up in-the-money. Along a path that rises from 100 to 200, the option struck at 100 was almost always in-the-money.

So think of an in-the-money option, in general. If the volatility of the underlying suddenly increases, what do you expect to happen to its probability of ending up in-the-money?

(a) It will go down.
(b) It will remain about the same.
(c) It will go up.

The probability should go down, because there is a greater chance that the stock will drop so far that it will actually go beneath the strike price.

If that doesn't make sense to you, think of the opposite: if the volatility falls drastically, say all the way to zero, what would happen to the probability of ending up in-the-money, if it is already in-the-money? The stock would no longer move, so naturally the probability would increase all the way to one.

If the intuition is not immediately obvious, you can hack it. Simply plot the sensitivity of the delta of a call option to the implied volatility as a function of the underlying price.

In the crazy language of option Greeks, this sensitivity is called "vanna," which, if you are a careful student of history and linguistics, you may recognize as having never in the history of the world been an actual Greek letter.

You may then rightly wonder why option "Greeks" are called that. You will then learn that there is no good reason.

In the world of Black-Scholes, vanna can be calculated equivalently as either the derivative of delta with respect to the volatility or the derivative of vega with respect to the spot price.

In general, though, all we really need to plot is the difference between the model delta and the market delta, literally the delta at a higher vol minus the delta at a lower vol. Figure 6.6 shows what it looks like as a function of the spot price.

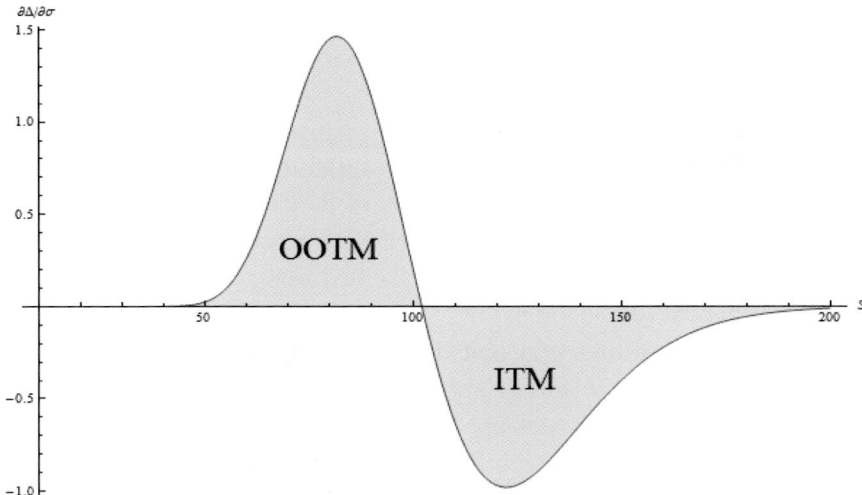

Figure 6.6. Vanna vs. underlying

The sensitivity of delta to vega is positive when the option is out-of-the-money and it is negative when the option is in-the-money. In other words, when you are hedging to a higher vol than the true vol, and your call is in-the-money, the delta you calculate will be smaller than it would have been if you had used the true vol.

So here's what's happening on paths that end up on high levels. You hold an in-the-money option. You hedge to a higher volatility than the truth. So your model delta is too low. You hedge by selling the model delta, but because it was too low, you did not sell enough of it to truly hedge yourself. Thus you are net long delta. And the market continues to climb. Along the whole path then, you are long the market, and the market is going up. Of course you end up making money.

That explains the right part of the heart.

The left part is similar. The paths that end up at the lowest final stock prices must have been falling the whole way. So your call option was out of the money the whole time. And because you were hedging to a higher than true vol, your delta was too high. You sold that delta; hence you were net short the market, and the market kept falling, so you again made money.

> "As a child, when I was having that alphabet soup, I never thought that it would pay off."
>
> *Vanna White*

So we've explained the left and right parts of the heart. What about the middle? There are two ways to think of it. The easy way is to note that so far we have not had any negative P&L at all, and so the middle should compensate for that, by being skewed towards losses. This is a reasonable way of looking at it.

The more complicated way gives a little bit more intuition. How can a volatile path end up where it started? Only if it is mean reverting, meaning that whenever it goes up, it tends to go back down the next day, and vice versa. Think of a path that constantly jumps between 102 and 98. At 102, your call is in the money, and you are net long delta because you are hedging to a higher-than-true vol. But then the market declines the next day, and so you lose money. At 98, your call is out of the money, and you are net short delta because you are hedging to a higher-than-true vol. But then the market soars the next day, and so you lose money. Each day, you lose money. That's why the middle is so pointy and lossy.

A final, somewhat oversimplified way of remembering the intuition is that as a trader you are betting that volatility will be high, that is to say, the stock will move far away from where it started. When it does that, you end up making money; when it doesn't, you lose money.

The upside-down heart when you hedge to a lower-than-true vol that appears in the second row of Figure 6.5 is not as sharply defined. Here, the true vol is 30 and your hedging vol is only 20. The reason the heart is less well-defined is because your error is more bounded. Let's walk through this logic.

When you are in-the-money, your 20-vol delta is typically above 0.5. Let's say on average it is about 0.75. Your 30-vol delta is going to be lower, and there is a lot of room for how much lower it can be; it can go all the way down to zero. Similarly, when you are out-of-the-money, your 20-vol delta is typically below 0.5. Let's say on average it is about

0.25. Your 30-vol delta is going to be higher, and there is a lot of room for how much higher it can be; it can go all the way up to one.

But now think if you are hedging to a lower vol, like in the second row of Figure 6.5 where the true vol is 30 and you are hedging to 20. When you are in-the-money, your 30-vol delta will be a little lower than in the above example, but let's say it averages about 0.7. The 20-vol delta will be higher, but there is not much room for how much higher it can be; the highest it can be is one. Similarly, when you are out-of-the-money, your 30-vol true delta will average about 0.3, and your 20-vol model delta will be lower, but there is not much room for how much lower it can be; the lowest it can be is zero. Thus, the difference between the model and the market delta is muted. It is still there, and you can still make out an upside-down heart, but it is less well-defined because the differences are smaller.

### 6.4.5 *The scatterplot of the P&L versus the realized vol*

Let's go back to the world where we hedge to the truth.

> "The truth is not for all men, but only for those who seek it."
>
> *Ayn Rand*

Look at the third column of plots in either the first or the fourth rows, i.e. where the hedge vol and simulation vol are either both 20 or both 30. It looks like the P&L from dynamically hedging an options position depends linearly on the realized volatility. The realized volatility, of course, is just the annualized standard deviation of the simulated log-returns.

If we believe Black-Scholes, shouldn't the P&L be randomly near zero? In other words, we can accept noise around the theoretical zero profit that we should see, noise coming from the failure to hedge perfectly continuously. But that noise should be random.

In the histogram, and in the scatterplot relative to the final stock price, it is indeed random: both overall and for any given final price, you are just as likely to make money as to lose money.

But when it comes to the realized volatility, it seems that the profit depends very heavily and very linearly. When the realized volatility is more than 22, you are guaranteed to make a profit, and when it is less than 18, you are guaranteed to lose.

Why does the P&L of a hedged options position depend so strongly and linearly on the realized volatility of the simulated path?

(a) Because the assumptions behind Black-Scholes are wrong.
(b) Because the derivation of Black-Scholes was wrong.
(c) Because we made an error in our simulation.
(d) It is just random. If we resimulate, it will go away.

The answer is none of the above. The anomaly is real and replicable.

> Monty Brewster: What are you gonna vote?
> Crowd: [in unison] None of the above!
>
> *Brewster's Millions* (1985)

At this point, you should object.

"Hold on," you should say. "We don't know ahead of time what the realized volatility will be. It is just as likely to end up at 22 and generate a profit as it is to end up at 18 and generate a loss. So it'll still be random."

Your statement is true. But remember that Black-Scholes claims that you should have zero profit along every single possible path. We can accommodate some noise due to discontinuous hedging, but that noise better be random and independent.

"Maybe it's the same error," you opine. "Maybe the discontinuous hedging is what is causing the realized volatility to differ from the true volatility."

Aha! You are right. If we look at thinner and thinner slices of returns, going from days to hours to minutes to seconds, the range of the possible realized volatility compresses. In the continuous limit, the realized volatility is always exactly 20.

So it is true that you cannot make money with the observation that the P&L is related to the realized volatility, because even if it has realized 22 after a few months, you don't know if the future realized volatility, being just another noisy draw from a population with a true vol of 20, will be above or below 20.

> "It ain't what you don't know that gets you into trouble. It's what you know for sure that just ain't so."
>
> *Mark Twain*

Here is why the P&L is positive for higher realized volatilities: it is because those paths are indistinguishable from paths generated from a higher true vol. Consider one specific path that was simulated from a 20 vol underlying but that randomly exhibited a realized vol of 22. That path could just as easily (more easily, really) come from a simulation of a 22 vol underlying.

Now, if you had a 22 vol underlying, and you hedged it to 20 vol, that would introduce some noise to your profit. But, on the other hand, you must have gotten a good deal on your initial options purchase, because you bought it at 20 implied vol, rather than at 22.

Thus the profit you have made is due to the 2 implied volatility point discount on the initial option, coupled with the noise from mishedging to the wrong vol. The explanation for the losses when the realized volatility is low is similar.

The short-form intuition is this: you bought a call and hedged it. So you are betting on higher volatility. When volatility ends up higher, even if only for random reasons, you benefit, and when it ends up lower, you lose.

That intuition continues to hold even if you hedge at the wrong vol. If, for example, the true vol is 30 but you hedge to 20, you are just introducing noise. The slope between your P&L and the realized vol is still positive, but not as sharply defined.

### 6.4.6 *The verdict and the missing piece of the puzzle*

So what's the answer? Should we hedge to model or to market?

There are two possibilities. If the model is correct, then we have seen above that hedging to the truth reduces the overall risk as well as the asymmetry depending on the final stock price. So if the model is also the truth, it seems we should hedge to the truth too. And if the market is the truth, then we should hedge to the market. Seems a little simplistic, doesn't it? Especially after all this work.

> "Ye shall know the truth, and the truth shall make you mad."
>
> *Aldous Huxley*

Three responses to that.

First, we know how just how much more risk hedging to the market is relative to the model, given that the model is right: it triples the hedging risks.

Second, we know what our risk looks like when we hedge to market instead of the true model: it looks like we are long a straddle, making more money when the underlying moves far away. This is already very useful.

But there is a third response, and that is that there is a wrinkle, something we have missed in all of the preceding analysis. What is this missing piece of the puzzle?

Is it the initial option price? Note that nowhere did we ask about what price we bought the option for. Could that be what is missing? If in one scenario we get a better deal, shouldn't that influence our decision?

No, because that has been assumed away. The question has been about how best to hedge an existing position, not whether to put it on or not. The position is on the books; how should you hedge it?

The question of what price you bought it at is irrelevant. The position has already been marked to market, so your initial execution brilliance or idiocy has already been accounted for.

That is why all of our graphs have been essentially centered around zero; the effect of buying the option cheaper would merely be to shift the center to a positive P&L without affecting any of the discussions about the risk.

The missing piece of the puzzle is the implicit assumption that all we care about is the terminal risk, the risk of our position at the end of its life.

Imagine you are a trader and you are holding a position in ten-year calls. The chances that you will still be at the same firm ten years from now is relatively small. Further, your bonus and your employment will be reviewed within one year, less than ten percent of the way into your option trade. The trade is not likely to converge by then.

What is the risk you are worried about? Is it really that your total P&L after ten years might have some noise on it? Or is it that your mark-to-market P&L may fluctuate?

> "Markets can remain irrational a lot longer than you and I can remain solvent."
>
> *A. Gary Shilling*

Of course, you are likely more worried about the mark-to-market P&L. From that perspective, does it make a difference whether you hedge to model or to market?

Yes, it does.

If the underlying goes up a dollar, the option price will go up by the market delta. That's nearly the definition of the market delta, and it follows exactly if the market implied volatility remains unchanged. If your hedge is not equal to the model delta, then you will experience some volatility in your mark-to-market P&L.

Thus, if you want to minimize your mark-to-market P&L, you may choose to hedge to the market even if you think the market volatility is wrong.

How do you trade-off these two risks, the mark-to-market risk versus the at-maturity risk? Ultimately, you probably will decide based on the maturity of the option you are hedging.

If the option will expire in a month or two, you will almost surely be able to weather any intermittent mark-to-market volatility, so you will lean towards hedging to model.

If the option will expire in many years, you will likely lean towards hedging to market, at least until the expiry gets closer.

And what do people do in practice? They hedge their bets on how to hedge.

One common rule of thumb is to hedge halfway between the model and the market delta. Then you're never exactly hedged, but you're never too far away either.

> "It is better to be vaguely right than exactly wrong."
> *Carveth Read*

# Part 3

# Exotic Derivatives

## Chapter 7

# Single-Asset Exotic Options

It is almost always easier to come up with a new kind of option than it is to price it. But constantly having to create new frameworks for pricing one-off opportunities means you will occasionally be too slow to participate in the potential profits. The lesson of this chapter is how to make substantial progress in understanding the character of an arbitrary exotic option with a few minutes of casual hacking rather than a few months of frantic research.

## 7.1 Introduction

Once you've worked your way up to be the head of your own trading desk, there will come a time when you begin hiring people to work for you. How can you identify the useful ones in the flood of interns and assistants that will besiege you? Or, if you are an intern or an assistant, how can you elevate yourself above your competitors?

One simple assignment you can give everybody is to have them explore and evaluate an exotic option. There are dozens of standard exotics and hundreds more that are customized to clients. You can pretty easily assign different exotics to each of the different people so that everyone has to do their own work.

And because most exotics do not have well-known, simple, closed-form solutions, this exercise will help you gauge both the creativity and the determination of the people you have tasked with the challenge. Some will do a passable job. Some will make subtle mistakes. Some will make gross mistakes and not even notice. Some will go the extra mile and look at things from a new angle.

Here, we are going to look at a wide range of exotics in a consistent framework. Recall our general simulation function:

```
Simulate[payoff_, n_ : 10 000, μ_ : 0, σ_ : .2, dt_ : 1/252, S0_ : 100, maturity_ : 1] :=
 payoff[FoldList[Times, S0, #]] & /@
  RandomReal[LogNormalDistribution[(μ - σ^2 / 2) dt, σ Sqrt@dt],
   {n, Ceiling[maturity / dt]}]
```

Given a payoff function that takes as input the list representing the stock price path and returns any number of values, we can tabulate the results across a variety of simulations. And we can then plot the results.

For example, to see the traditional payoff diagram of a plain vanilla at-the-money call, we can define the payoff function to return both the last price in the path and the intrinsic value of the option, and then plot the latter against the former:

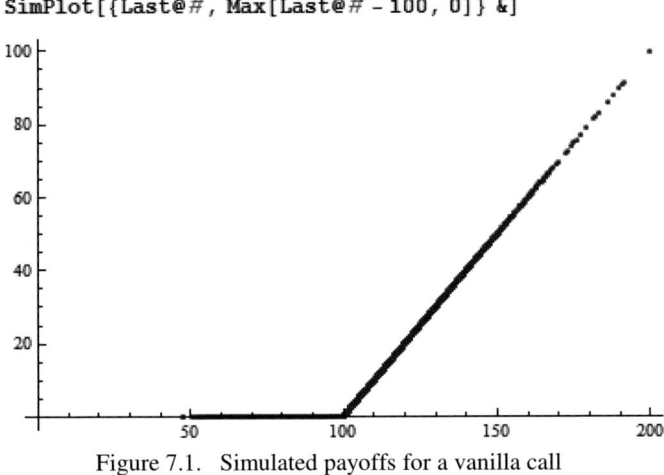

Figure 7.1. Simulated payoffs for a vanilla call

The "slot notation" in Mathematica using "#" to refer to the argument and "&" to mark the end of the function definition lets you define quick, in-line functions.

SimPlot is just defined for convenience as a function that plots either the result of a simulation given a payoff function, or the given results themselves. (It is defined in this general way to accommodate graphing multiple outputs on the same plot.)

Specifically, the code for SimPlot is primarily just a wrapper for the built-in function ListPlot:

```
SepCols[list_] := If[Length@Dimensions@list == 2,
   Table[list[[All, {1, n}]], {n, 2, Last@Dimensions@list}], list]
SimPlot[payoff_Function] := SimPlot[Simulate[payoff]];
SimPlot[data_List] :=
 With[{vals = SepCols[data]},
   ListPlot[vals, PlotRange -> All, AxesOrigin -> {0, 0},
     PlotStyle -> Opacity[If[Length@vals == 1, 1, .4]]]]
```

where the PlotRange and AxesOrigin parameter choices are to make sure we see all of the generated points on a standard axis, and SepCols is a helper function used in case we want to plot more than one result simultaneously.

Once again, Mathematica is not necessary. Much the same results could be obtained with R, where functions can also be passed as arguments.

You could even do this all in Excel by simulating the paths once and defining a single column as the payoff, changing its definition for each exotic option.

The primary benefit of Mathematica is its brevity; even if you don't know the language, you can understand the logic.

Mathematica also includes substantial built-in financial engineering functions including pricing algorithms and sensitivity analyses for dozens of exotic options. Other pricers are available for Excel and R and other languages, as well as standalone packages and interfaces through Bloomberg terminals.

But those are not what are important here. The purpose of this chapter is not to price any or even all of the exotic options listed here. It is instead to show how a little simple financial hacking can go a long way towards understanding. These examples are just that — examples. The goal is to be able to quickly gain intuition about new derivatives for which no pricing algorithm has yet been written.

## 7.2 Binary Asset-or-Nothing

An asset-or-nothing call pays off the entire asset if it is above the strike, and zero otherwise. Compare that with the vanilla call which pays off the difference between the asset and the strike if it is in-the-money.

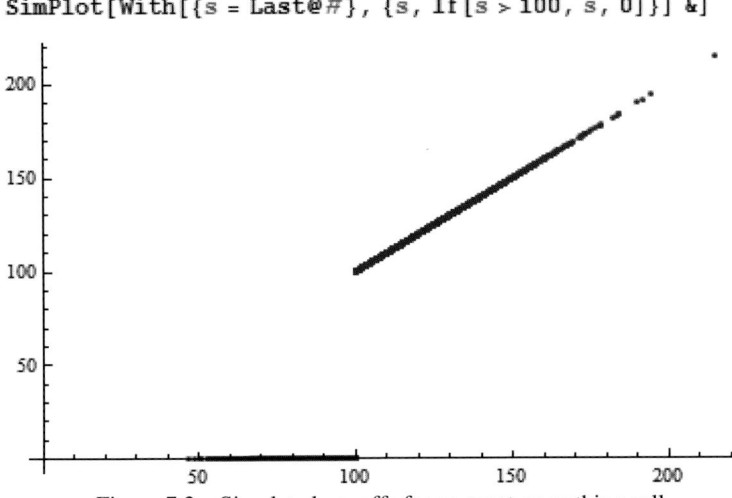

Figure 7.2. Simulated payoffs for an asset-or-nothing call

The biggest change is the discontinuity at the strike price. With a plain vanilla call, you don't care if the underlying ends exactly at the strike or a millionth of a penny above the strike; with an asset-or-nothing call, that tiny difference could net you $100.

Notice that here, as with the plain vanilla call, there are almost no points below $50 or above $200. This is because our standard assumptions, particularly of 20 vol, make it very hard for a simulation to move that far away from its initial price. You can see that above about $175, the dots thin out. They are far less numerous there.

An asset-or-nothing call is not the only kind of asset-or-nothing option. You can just as easily have an asset-or-nothing put, as shown in Figure 7.3.

```
SimPlot[With[{s = Last@#}, {s, If[s < 100, s, 0]}] &]
```

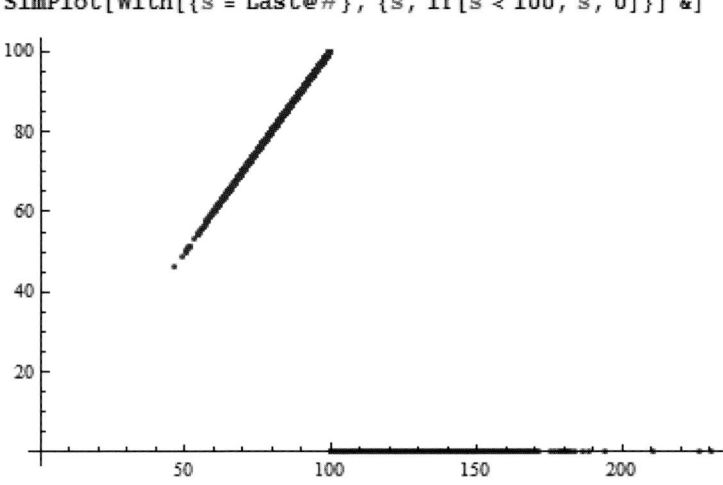

Figure 7.3. Simulated payoffs for an asset-or-nothing put

But note that the asset-or-nothing put has even less in common with a vanilla put than the asset-or-nothing call has with a vanilla call. Not only is there a discontinuity when the spot price is near the strike, but the slope of the payoff is now opposite to that of its vanilla equivalent.

Indeed, although our simulations don't have enough volatility to reach there, the payoff continues sloping down all the way to zero. So you might conjecture that an asset-or-nothing put is the same as holding the asset minus a plain vanilla at-the-money call. But that doesn't quite work out. You need to also lose an extra $100 if the asset ends up above $100, and that doesn't lend itself easily to manipulations with plain vanilla options.

It's very common that no static combinations of plain vanilla options result in exotic options payoffs. That may well be the best definition of exotic options. After all, straddles or bull spreads are not really exotic options; they are just options positions.

However, it is equally true that exotic options are often combinations of other exotic options. For example, what if you combine a long position in the asset (or, equivalently in terms of payoff, a long forward struck at zero) with a short asset-or-nothing call? That would generate the same payoff as an asset-or-nothing put:

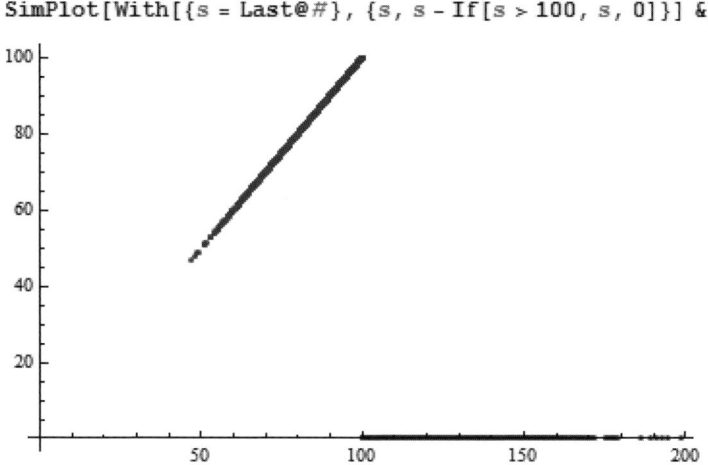

Figure 7.4.  Simulated payoffs for a long asset and a short asset-or-nothing call

And we can see why: if the asset exceeds $100, the payoff is zero, but if it falls short of $100, the payoff is the value of the asset, matching the definition of the asset-or-nothing put.

One needs to be careful with specifics of each particular exotic, but in general, it is common that even exotic puts and calls satisfy some version of the put-call parity. It won't necessarily be the same as the vanilla relationship, but there will usually be some static replication relationship between the two. It is a good idea to try to do that for every kind of exotic option listed in this chapter, or that you encounter in real life.

The vanilla put-call parity is that the combination of a long call and a short put are a forward; here, the combination of a long asset-or-nothing call and a long asset-or-nothing put are a forward struck at zero.

Why? Because no matter where the asset ends up, exactly one of your asset-or-nothing options pays off, and it pays off with the asset.

## 7.3  Binary Cash-or-Nothing

The complement to an asset-or-nothing call is a cash-or-nothing call, often called a digital or a binary call.

## Single-Asset Exotic Options

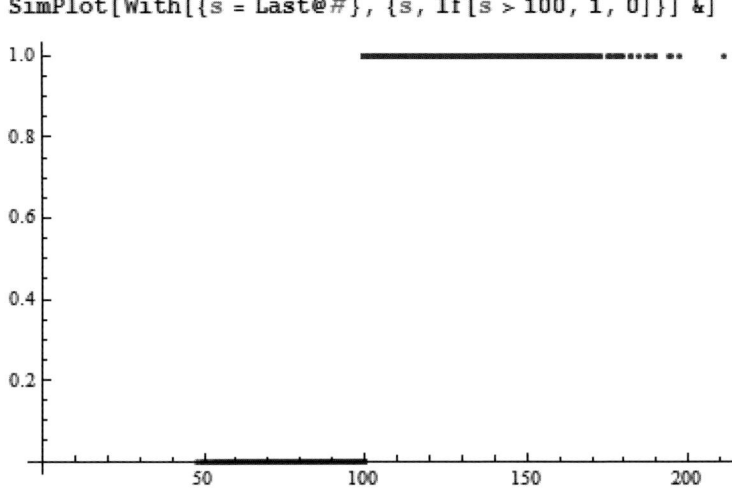

Figure 7.5. Simulated payoffs for a cash-or-nothing call

The cash-or-nothing put is one minus the cash-or-nothing call:

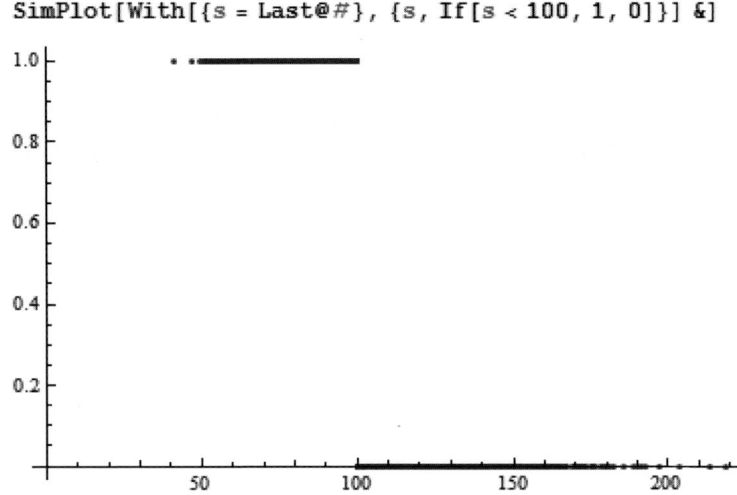

Figure 7.6. Simulated payoffs for a cash-or-nothing put

Naturally, combinations of any two of plain vanilla options, asset-or-nothing options, and cash-or-nothing options can replicate the third: e.g., a vanilla call is an asset-or-nothing call minus $K$ cash-or-nothing calls.

## 7.4 Barrier Options

There are four types of barrier options, so it is easiest to discuss them all at once. Barriers can be up or down, and in or out. The direction (up or down) refers to where the barrier is relative to the initial underlying price. The knock (in or out) refers to whether the barrier brings an option to life or extinguishes it.

For example, an up-and-in barrier call is not exercisable until the underlying first rises to the barrier level. A down-and-out barrier put is exercisable only so long as the underlying does not first drop to the barrier level. And similarly for the rest.

Here are simulation results for an up-and-out call with a 150 barrier:

`SimPlot[With[{s = Last@#}, {s, If[Max@# > 150, 0, Max[s - 100, 0]]}] &]`

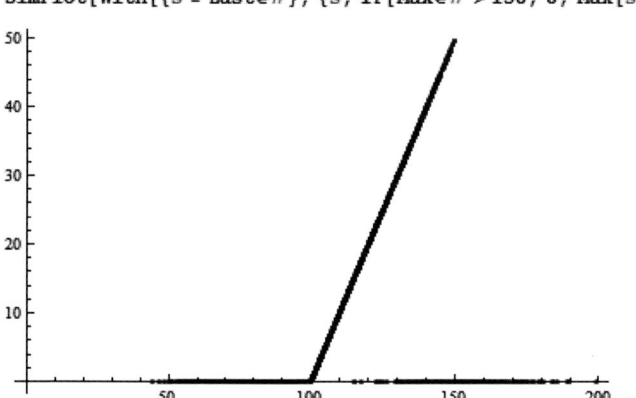

Figure 7.7. Simulated payoffs for an up-and-out call

Notice that any path that ends above 150 will necessarily pay out zero because the barrier was breached and the option was extinguished. And of course the payoff is also zero if the final price is below the strike price, regardless of whether the barrier had been reached, because the option expires out of the money. But for final stock prices between 100 and 150, some paths pay out zero and some pay out the intrinsic value. The difference depends on whether the barrier was hit or not on those particular paths.

Thus the graph of the up-and-out call is like a vanilla call but with some points dropped to zero. So obviously the price of an up-and-out call must be less than the price of a vanilla call. The difference in the price is how much of a discount you need to take the risk that your option will be extinguished by the barrier.

The payout function for a barrier option can be generalized to: if the max or min is greater or less than the barrier, then you get the option.

| Barrier Style | You get the option if: |
| --- | --- |
| Up-and-In | Max > Barrier |
| Up-and-Out | Max < Barrier |
| Down-and-In | Min < Barrier |
| Down-and-Out | Min > Barrier |

## 7.5 Restrike Options

An example of a restrike call would be a call struck at $100 whose strike price falls to $75 if the underlying ever falls below $85. Here's what a simulation of such a payoff would look like:

`SimPlot[With[{s = Last@#}, {s, Max[s - If[Min@# < 85, 75, 100], 0]}] &]`

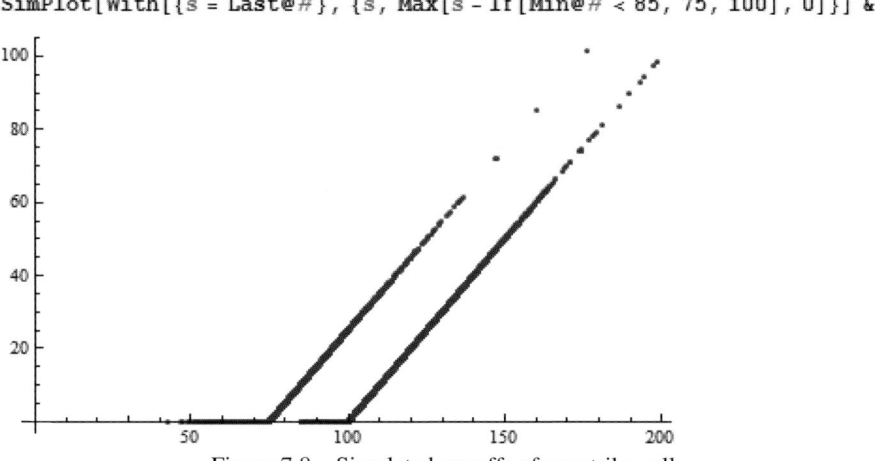

Figure 7.8. Simulated payoffs of a restrike call

It almost looks like two separate options, one struck at $100 and one struck at $75, where the probability you get the lower-struck option declines with the terminal price. You can imagine the similar graph for a restrike put.

Can we replicate a restrike option with combinations of asset-or-nothing, cash-or-nothing, and barrier options?

There are two ways to think about such questions: graphically and algebraically. When we proved put-call parity, it was easier to think about it graphically. In this case, because the payout depends on the maximum along the path, it is probably easier to approach it algebraically.

The only other exotic payoff we have seen so far to use the maximum is a barrier. But which kind? First let's try to rewrite the restrike call payoff to look more like a barrier payoff:

$$\text{Max}[s - \text{If}[\text{MinPrice} < 85, 75, 100], 0]$$
$$= \text{If}[\text{MinPrice} < 85, \text{Max}[s - 75, 0], \text{Max}[s - 100, 0]]$$

where the convenient $\text{If}[test, trueval, falseval]$ expression evaluates to $trueval$ if $test$ is true and to $falseval$ if $test$ is false.

We can rewrite the last line as the sum of two barrier options, a down-and-in and a down-and-out, but with different strikes:

$$\text{If}[\text{MinPrice} < 85, \text{Max}[s - 75, 0], 0]$$
$$+ \text{If}[\text{MinPrice} > 85, \text{Max}[s - 100, 0], 0]$$

If the minimum price is less than the 85 barrier, then you get a call struck at 75. If the minimum price is above the 85 barrier, then you get a call struck at 100. So our specific restrike call is just the sum of a down-and-in 85-barrier 75-strike call and a down-and-out 85-barrier 100-strike call.

Notice that a financial mathematician would have used variables for the various strikes and barriers, but as financial hackers we do not bother. We have a much better intuition of what the 75, 85, and 100 mean, and are less likely to confuse them, than we are if we call them $K_R$, $B$, and $K$.

And besides, we squeezed out every last bit of intuition.

Similar replication logic would apply to restrike puts or different values of the parameters. Usually restrike options only restrike favorably to the option holder, so the strike can only get lowered for calls and raised for puts, but the same logic could work even for restrike options that could restrike against the option holder.

> "Dammit Smithers, this isn't rocket science, it's brain surgery!"
>
> *C. Montgomery Burns*, "The Simpsons" (1991)

## 7.6 Lookback Options and Range Options

There are two types of lookback options: fixed-strike and floating-strike. Both types pay off the highest possible intrinsic value, but they do it either by making the strike price be the best it could have been, or by making the underlying value be the best it could have been.

A fixed-strike lookback call pays off the positive difference between the highest price along the path and the strike: $\text{Max}[0, MaxPrice - K]$. A floating-strike lookback call pays off the difference between the final underlying value and the lowest price along the path: $S_T - MinPrice$. The payoffs of lookback puts are similarly defined.

With the mild adjustment discussed in Section 7.1 to SimPlot to allow for multiple values, we can see both types of lookback calls together:

```
SimPlot[With[{s = Last@#}, {s, Max@# - 100, s - Min@#}] &]
```

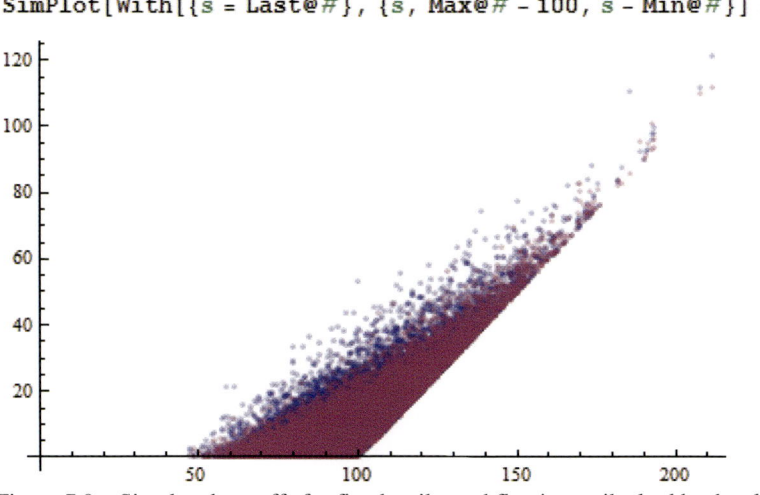

Figure 7.9. Simulated payoffs for fixed-strike and floating-strike lookback calls

Both of them are always at least as good as the plain vanilla, but the fixed-strike payoffs seem to dominate the floating-strike payoffs. Why?

Look at the range of terminal values. The underlying is always between 50 and 200. So the most you can get with a fixed-strike lookback call is 200-100, and the most you can get with a floating-strike lookback call is 100-50. That's why the former seems to dominate.

A floating-strike lookback call and a fixed-strike lookback call struck at the initial underlying price $S_0$, combined with a short forward struck at $S_0$, pays off $MaxPrice - MinPrice$. This is known as a range option.

## 7.7 Asian Options

Asian options are just like lookback options except instead of taking the most extreme value along the path, we take the average. There are again two styles: fixed-strike and floating-strike.

The averaging period need not be the entire history. For example, a fixed-strike Asian call can define the averaging only over the last few days or weeks.

The following plot shows the two possible kinds of Asian calls:

```
SimPlot[With[{s = Last@#},
    {s, Max[s - Mean@#, 0], Max[Mean[#[[-10 ;;]]] - 100, 0]}] &]
```

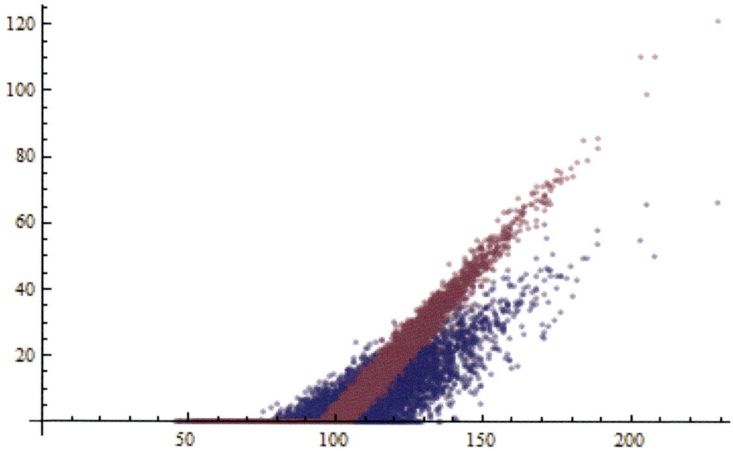

Figure 7.10. Simulated payoffs for floating-strike and fixed-strike Asian calls

Each type looks like a noisy vanilla call, the noise coming from the fact that the average can be either higher or lower than the final value.

The fixed-strike Asian call in the example is averaged over just the final 10 days, so its noise is much lower.

Note also that the slope of the floating-strike Asian call is much lower. When the final stock price is $150 as opposed to $100, the average payoff is only about $25 more, rather than $50 more. Why?

Because for the final stock price to be $150, having started from $100, the average price would only be about $125.

## 7.8 Chooser Options

A chooser option lets you decide at some point at or before the moment of exercise whether your option was a put or a call. If you can only choose at expiry, then the chooser is identical to a straddle.

The graph below shows the payoff of a chooser when you must decide after six months whether you want the option on the remaining six months to be a put or a call. Presumably you will make your decision depending on whether the price at that time is above or below the strike.

```
SimPlot[With[{s = Last@#},
    {s, If[#[[126]] > 100, Max[s - 100, 0], Max[100 - s, 0]]}] &]
```

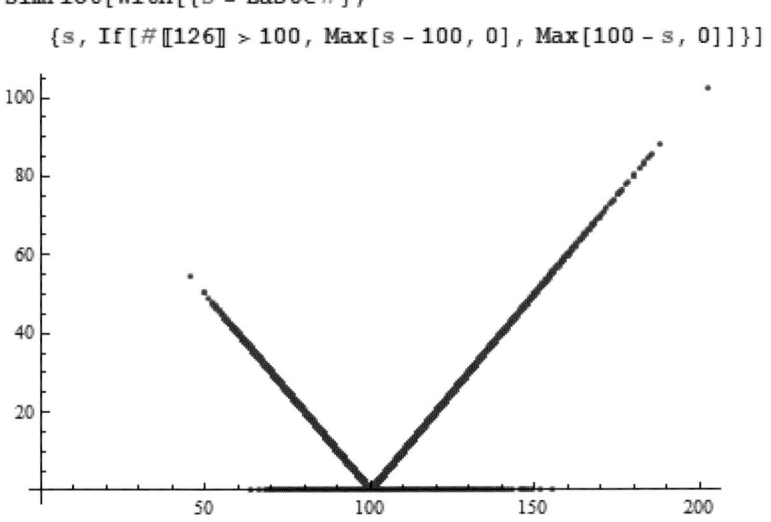

Figure 7.11. Simulated payoffs for a six-month into six-month chooser

Compared to a straddle, there are many more points that pay off zero, along paths where the underlying reversed course after six months. The plot below shows the percentage of zero chooser payoffs depending on the moment of choice. If you must choose on day 1, then, like vanilla options, about half the paths expire worthless. Halfway through, about a quarter of the paths expire worthless.

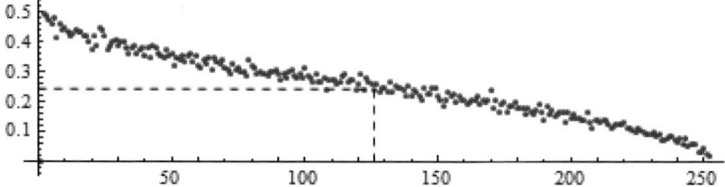

Figure 7.12.  Percentage of zero chooser payoffs vs. days before choice

## 7.9  Cliquet Options

A one-year cliquet call with monthly resets pays off the sum of 12 monthly options with strikes equal to the preceding month-end values. So they are also the sum of 12 one-year restrike calls that restrike at the end of each month. Cliquet options are also called ratchet options.

```
SimPlot[{Last@#,
    Total[Differences[#[[ ;; ;; 21]]] /. n_ /; n < 0 → 0]} &]
```

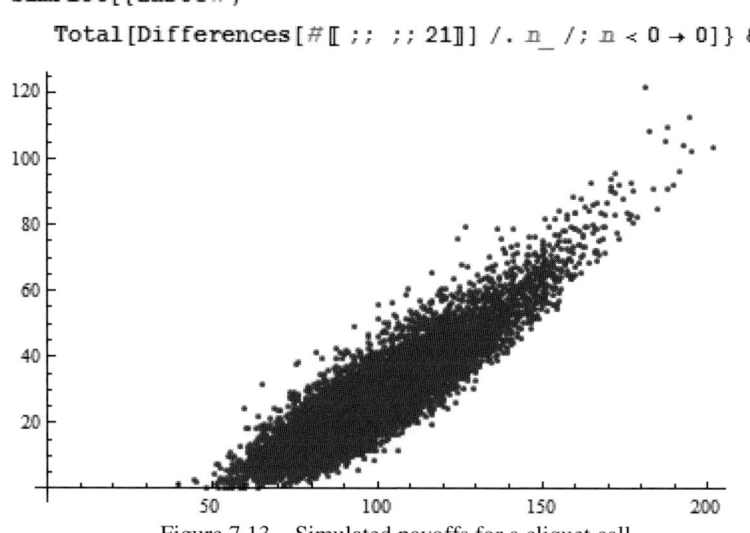

Figure 7.13.  Simulated payoffs for a cliquet call

Such options are among the most difficult to model, hedge, or gain intuition about. But following the same principles as we've seen in the rest of this chapter, we can hack out some intuition in one line of code.

The code and the result are shown in Figure 7.13 on the previous page. This single-line payoff function calculates the 21-day rolling differences, replaces all negative values with zeros, and plots the total as a function of the final stock price. You can still make money even if the terminal stock price is low because there will likely be at least one positive month out of twelve.

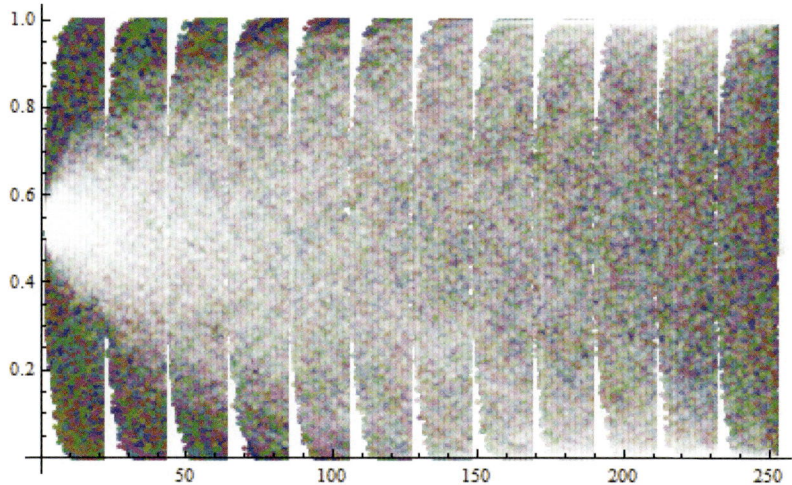

Figure 7.14. Cliquet delta and vanilla call delta

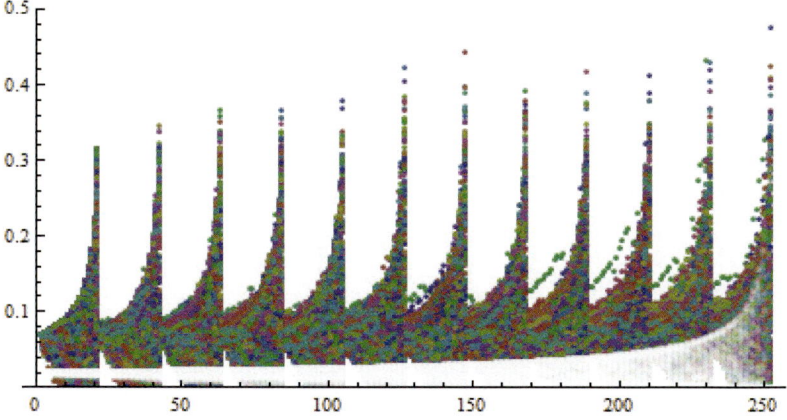

Figure 7.15. Cliquet gamma and vanilla call gamma

Because of their resets, cliquet deltas return to the delta of an at-the-money call each month, approximately 0.51 for our parameters. Figure 7.14 shows the delta of the cliquet on a thousand simulated paths, overlayed in white with the delta of a plain vanilla one-year call.

You can see the cliquet deltas being reset monthly, whereas the plain vanilla call delta starts at about 0.54 and spreads out to the edges over time, finishing of course either at zero or at one at maturity.

Even more striking than the difference in deltas is the difference in gammas shown in Figure 7.15. Cliquets have far more gamma.

# Chapter 8

# Multi-Asset Exotic Options

Every option whose payoff depends on more than one underlying is an exotic option. This is the center of some of the most interesting recent innovations in the derivatives world.

## 8.1 Introduction

Single-asset options at first seemed to be about exposure to the underlying, but turned out to be basically all about volatility. Multi-asset options at first seem to be about complex combinations of exposures to various underlyings, but will turn out to be basically all about correlation.

Of course, the preceding paragraph is false. Options are about more than one thing, by definition. But to the extent it is useful to think of single-asset options as being primarily about volatility (in addition to the underlying exposure), it is almost as useful to think of multi-asset options as being primarily about correlation (in addition to the individual volatilities and underlying exposures).

So let's start with an example. Is an option on a portfolio or an index such as the S&P 500 a multi-asset option?

  (a) Yes, because there is more than one asset in the index. For example, there are 500 components in the S&P 500.
  (b) No, because the S&P 500 has an associated futures contract that can be used to hedge the underlying.
  (c) It depends on whether the option is a vanilla call or put, or an exotic option such as a barrier or a cliquet.

The answer is none of the above. Such an option is not a multi-asset option, so (b) is closest to correct, but the reason given is wrong. The option would still be only a single-asset option even if it was on a custom portfolio, such as two shares of Google and three shares of IBM, which does not have an associated futures contract.

The way to tell if an option is effectively on a single asset or on multiple assets is to look at the payoff function and see if it depends only on a single linear combination of holdings in the multiple assets. If it does, then it is just an option on a portfolio, and it can be either a vanilla option or an exotic single-asset option. If the payoff cannot be expressed in terms of a single linear combination of the individual assets, then you are dealing with a real live multi-asset option, and all multi-asset options are exotic options.

Specifically, a multi-asset option can have different payouts even when the portfolio value is the same; a single-asset vanilla option always has just one payout for a given portfolio value; and a single-asset exotic option always has just own payout for a given portfolio path.

## 8.2 Spread Options

A spread option depends on the difference between two assets. An IBM-MSFT spread call with a strike of zero, for example, pays out the excess of IBM's price over MSFT's price at maturity, if that number is positive.

Is a spread option a multi-asset option?

(a) No, because as we just discussed above, the payout depends only on a fixed combination of the two assets. Specifically, the underlying can be replicated by buying one share of IBM and shorting one share of MSFT. So we are left with just an option on that spread, and we know there need not be an associated futures for that particular linear combination. Thus, a spread option is just a run-of-the-mill single-asset option in disguise.

(b) Yes, because it is in this chapter on multi-asset exotic options.

The answer is almost (b). It is a multi-asset option, but not merely because it is in this chapter.

A spread option is not a single-asset option because, although it does depend on a fixed linear combination of two assets, that linear combination contains negative numbers, and is therefore not a long portfolio.

Why is such a subtle distinction important here?

Because a portfolio of long positions in various securities, each of which is lognormally distributed, is itself at least approximately lognormally distributed. (It is not exactly lognormally distributed, a fact which troubles financial mathematicians to no end, but is shrugged off by financial hackers who recognize that even individual securities are not really lognormally distributed either. It is all approximations anyway.)

But a spread between two lognormal securities is almost definitely not lognormally distributed. Why?

Because the difference can be negative. A lognormal distribution does not allow negative numbers. Stock prices are well-modeled as lognormal because they cannot be negative. But the difference between two stock prices may indeed be negative, with substantial probability.

We can introduce a new multi-asset simulation function that extends our single-asset simulation function by drawing from $k$ multinormal random variables distributed identically with zero mean and 20 percent annualized standard deviation. We will assume that all pairwise correlations between different assets are the same parameter value $\rho$.

```
SimulateMulti[payoff_, k_, ρ_ : 0, n_ : 10 000, μ_ : 0, σ_ : .2, dt_ : 1/252, S0_ : 100,
    maturity_ : 1] := payoff[FoldList[Times, ConstantArray[S0, k], 1 + #]] & /@
   RandomVariate[MultinormalDistribution[ConstantArray[μ dt, k],
     Table[If[i == j, 1, ρ] σ^2 dt, {i, k}, {j, k}]], {n, Ceiling[maturity/dt]}]
```

Figure 8.1 shows the payoff of a spread call with a zero strike between two identical securities for $\rho = -0.9$ and $\rho = +0.9$, as a function of the long asset's terminal price.

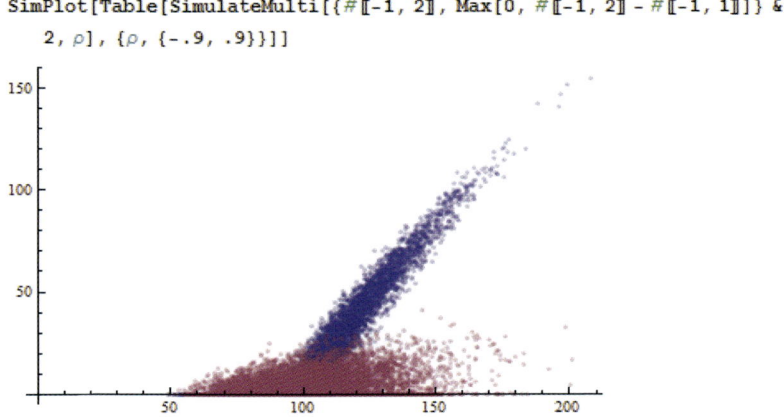

Figure 8.1. Simulated payoffs for spread calls with high and low correlations

When the correlation is significantly negative, the spread call begins to resemble a vanilla call. When the correlation is significantly positive, it begins to look more random. Why?

For a very negative correlation, the spread is essentially equal to twice the long asset: $L - S \approx L - (-L) = 2L$. That's why the slope of the points for the negative correlation is twice that of a vanilla call: when the long underlying is at 150, the spread pays off not just the 50 that a vanilla call would, but 100.

For a very positive correlation, the spread is essentially equal to zero: $L - S \approx L - L = 0$. There is still some randomness, so there are occasional positive payouts. If there were a nonzero strike, the payouts would be squeezed even closer to zero.

Different formulations of spread options can lead to different closed form formulas or computational techniques for determining the relevant pricing and hedging. But our goal here is not to review such methodologies. The known techniques change, and can be found elsewhere. Indeed, Mathematica for example now has built-in support for pricing many exotic options. Developing new and more efficient techniques is always a useful research endeavor, but it is not financial hacking.

Our focus in this section, indeed in this chapter and in the book overall, is to build intuition so that we can quickly gain deep understanding of even brand new products, faster than the competition. To that end, we don't look to find delicate new pricing formulas, but rather rigorous and useful ways of looking at the problem.

For example, spread options are typically valued using a change of numeraire approach that is quite clever and interesting. The idea behind it is that you imagine that assets in the economy are priced not relative to cash, but to another asset, specifically the second asset in the spread option. This is an incredibly useful approach that can be extended to developing explicit pricing formulas for many other kinds of options.

So why do I omit teaching it to you here? Because it only applies to certain kinds of options. And the options and derivatives I want you to be able to tackle are those that occur in the real world. And in the real world, options and derivatives are never limited to what can be elegantly priced.

## 8.3 Outperformance Options

Outperformance options are similar to spread options except instead of looking at the difference between two assets, it focuses on the ratio. The graph looks almost identical except for a different $y$-axis, so there is no reason to reproduce it, but the value of outperformance options specifically lies in its usefulness in certain kinds of trades.

Outperformance options turn out to be especially useful in the context of relative value A/B share class trades like the ones discussed in Chapter 3. Suppose the A shares cost two percent more than the B shares, and that this is not enough to entice you to sell short the A's and buy the B's, but that when the discrepancy hits five percent, you will want to put on the trade.

The naïve approach is to sit and wait and hope that it hits five percent. If it does, you start slowly putting on the position, trying to minimize your transactions costs while crossing your fingers that the spread doesn't collapse before you are finished entering. If it never reaches five percent, then you do nothing.

What can you do with a tool like outperformance options? You can sell the option on the return difference! Suppose you sell a European option with a three-month maturity and a strike of five percent. If at the end of three months the discrepancy exceeds five percent, your counterparty will exercise it, because you would owe them any difference over and above the five percent. But from your perspective, this is great, because you would have tried to enter the trade at a five percent mispricing anyway, and with an option, you are able to enter without transactions costs, in large size, and in the perfect ratio, all at once.

In other words, here are your choices. Without an outperformance option, if the spread at the end of three months is say seven percent, then you are likely facing a mark-to-market loss of two percent plus your transactions costs to enter the trade. With the outperformance option, you are facing a loss of two percent exactly; plus the shares you trade with your counterparty were not the result of trading on a listed exchange so you may have more confidentiality in your position.

But that's not all.

> "But wait, there's more!"
>
> *Ron Popeil*

What if the discrepancy never exceeds five percent? Then without an outperformance option, you gain nothing and lose nothing. You were never in the trade.

But with an outperformance option, you keep the original premium that you were paid for selling it. And you can do it over and over again.

## 8.4 Rainbow Options

A rainbow option pays off one of the colors of a rainbow, if you happen to live in a world where rainbows refract assets instead of light. They are more commonly known as "best-of" or "worst-of" options.

The payoff of a best-of at-the-money call on two identical assets is the maximum of their terminal values minus their average initial price. Figure 8.2 plots this payoff as a function of the correlation, ranging from -0.50 to +0.50 in increments of 0.25. It also plots the points representing the average payoff for each given correlation.

## Multi-Asset Exotic Options

```
With[{vals = Table[SimulateMulti[{Correlation[Returns@#][[1, 2]],
      Max[Max[Last@#] - 100, 0]} &, 2, ρ, 10000],
    {ρ, -1/2, 1/2, 1/4}]},
  Show[SimPlot[vals], ListLinePlot[Mean /@ vals,
    PlotMarkers → Graphics[{Red, PointSize[Medium], Point[{0, 0}]}],
    PlotStyle → White],
   Epilog → {White, Inset[Last@#, #, {0, 2}] & /@ (Mean /@ vals)}]]
```

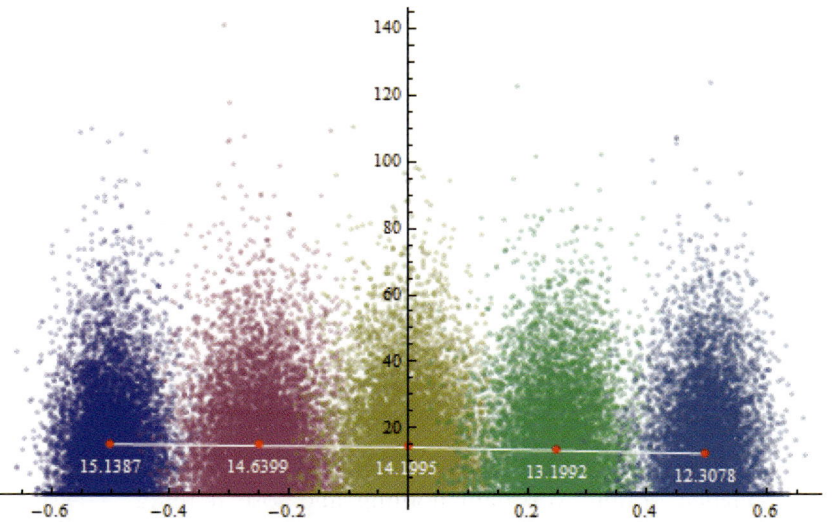

Figure 8.2. Simulated payoffs for a rainbow call paying off the best of two assets

Notice the code looks more complicated now. Actually, the code for plotting the payoffs would still be one line: it would simply be SimPlot[vals], where vals is defined in the With clause.

The rest of the code is for plotting as red points the average payoffs for each value of the correlation and connecting them with a white line.

The first thing to notice is the colorful blobs. They seem to simply be random noise, no matter what the correlation is.

But on second look, the red points clearly decrease with higher correlation. As the two securities resemble each other more and more, the value of the best-of option decreases. This makes sense. When the correlation hits one, you are really just long a regular call option.

How can we think about the real-world performance of hedged rainbow options? After all, here we may potentially have to delta hedge in each of the assets underlying the rainbow option.

We can shed some light on the subject very simply, by looking at simulated paths of 252 days and seeing, on each day, how many of the underlying assets are within five percent of the best performing asset to date. Figure 8.3 plots this for nine simulations of five identical assets each. Each dot in each simulation represents whether that particular asset on that particular day in that particular simulation was within five percent of the best performing asset in that simulation on that day.

```
GraphicsColumn[
 Table[
  ArrayPlot[
   Transpose@
    First@SimulateMulti[
     With[{th = 0.95 Max[#]}, With[{c = Count[#, n_ /; n > th]},
      If[# > th, 1/c, 0] & /@ #]] & /@ # &, 5, 0, 1], ImageSize → 600,
    Frame → False, PixelConstrained → {6, 5}], {9}], Frame → All, Spacings → 10,
  Epilog → {Inset[Style[ToString@#, 10], {-3, 20 - 40 #}] & /@ Range[9]}]
```

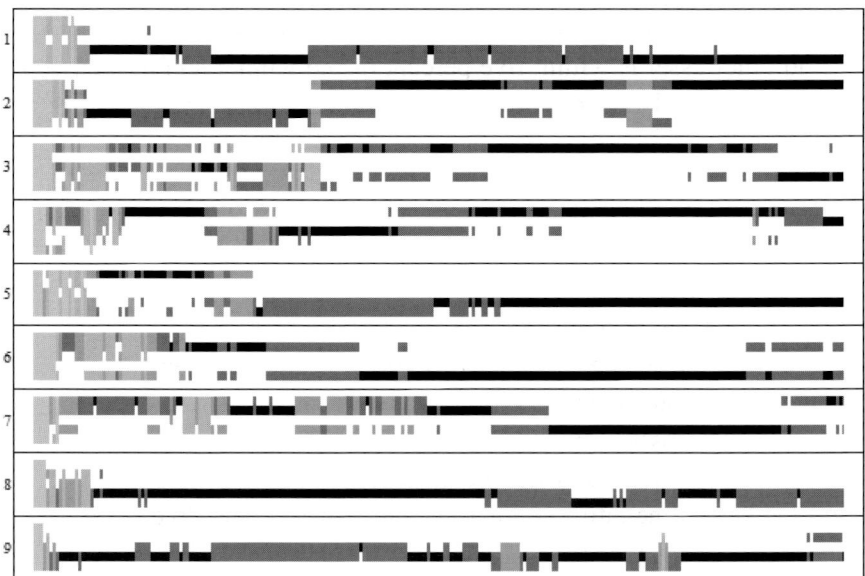

Figure 8.3. A quick approximation to the deltas of a rainbow call on five identical assets

Initially, all five assets are of course equal, and so all of them are within five percent of each other.

But you can see in most cases, there come about long periods where there is just one winner. The fewer assets there are within five percent of the best, the darker their spots, until when there is just one left, such as the end of scenario 5, there is just a straight black line.

Of course, the best performer can change. Notice in scenario 7 how the second asset had a long run being the best, with intermittent challenges from the first asset, but then the fourth asset took over, and even later the first asset came back again and ultimately won.

Notice further that during the changeover, both were at some point within five percent of the best. Those dots represent a very quick approximation to the delta of each security.

"How? Why?" you gasp. You may be surprised. Let's walk through it.

> Hansen: Scared?
> Nash: Terrified. Mortified. Petrified. Stupefied. By you.
>
> *A Beautiful Mind* (2001)

If no other asset is within five percent of the winner so far, then your exposure is virtually entirely just to that asset. If it goes up, your rainbow call is worth more, the same as a vanilla call on a single asset.

But suppose there are two assets, neck and neck. Then you basically have equal exposure to both of them, and as one races ahead, you will want to buy more of it, and sell the loser.

This is the relative value trading that will ultimately decide the cost of replicating this exotic option. If there is cross-sectional momentum in the assets, so that the winners continue to go up while the losers continue to go down, then your hedging will make you money, or at least not lose. But if there is cross-sectional mean reversion, so that the winning asset keeps switching, then you will be constantly buying high and selling low. That's the kind of negative gamma that can drive a trader to despair.

But fortunately, we are able to capture the essence of this trade in just these few quick graphs. Meanwhile, if you were to try to derive a complete closed-form solution to this asset, it would take you months, if not years, at which point the pricing would have stabilized, the opportunity would have vanished, and the hot money would have moved on to yet another kind of derivative. Alternatively, if you were more of a fly-by-the-seat-of-your-pants kind of trader with little regard for models or even hacking, you might think it is a good trade and not notice the potential danger.

Financial hacking gives you the best combination, in my humble opinion. You are able to quickly price a brand-new derivative, evaluate its hedging shortcomings, and perhaps most importantly, potentially negotiate with the counterparty offering the derivative to incorporate a different group of assets.

From the counterparty's perspective, they may not even recognize the implicit dependence on the cross-sectional relationships. They may be perfectly willing to examine a different portfolio of assets. And that different portfolio may be far less likely to cause you a hedging nightmare.

# Part 4

# Exotic Worlds

Chapter 9

# The Best Trade in the World?

An exotic world is one where the Black-Scholes assumptions break down, particularly the assumption about constant volatility. Unfortunately, when that assumption breaks down, so do a lot of our intuitions. This chapter's goal is to build your intuitions back up so that you will not fall victim to fake arbitrage opportunities. It is centered on trying to convince you of the discovery of the best trade in the world. It is up to you to debunk the claims.

## 9.1 Introduction

So far we have assumed that the true volatility of the underlying asset, or assets, has been constant. The realized volatility has noise, but only because we simulate on non-continuous time intervals such as on a daily basis; the noise diminishes for smaller time intervals.

In such a constant underlying volatility world, what would the implied volatility of one-year options struck at $90 or $110 look like?

(a) They would be the same.
(b) They would be different from each other.

The correct answer is we don't know, because the implied volatility of an option is just a non-linear transformation of its market price, and the market price can in principle be anything.

The implied volatility, if you recall, is just that particular value for the volatility parameter of Black-Scholes that spits out the market price when plugged into the Black-Scholes pricing formula alongside the strike and maturity of the option, the value of the underlying, and the interest rate and dividend yield.

But in a world with no arbitrage opportunities, the correct answer is (a). Another way of putting it is that in a world where you have no limits on your ability to pursue arbitrage opportunities, you and people like you would eventually push the market prices of options such that their implied volatilities were all the same, and equaled the true underlying volatility. You would do this by buying the options with low implied volatility, selling the options with high implied volatility, and hedging all of your positions to the true volatility.

The figure below shows a few possible stylized examples of what we might see in a real-world market if we plot the implied volatilities of options for a given underlying and maturity as a function of their strikes.

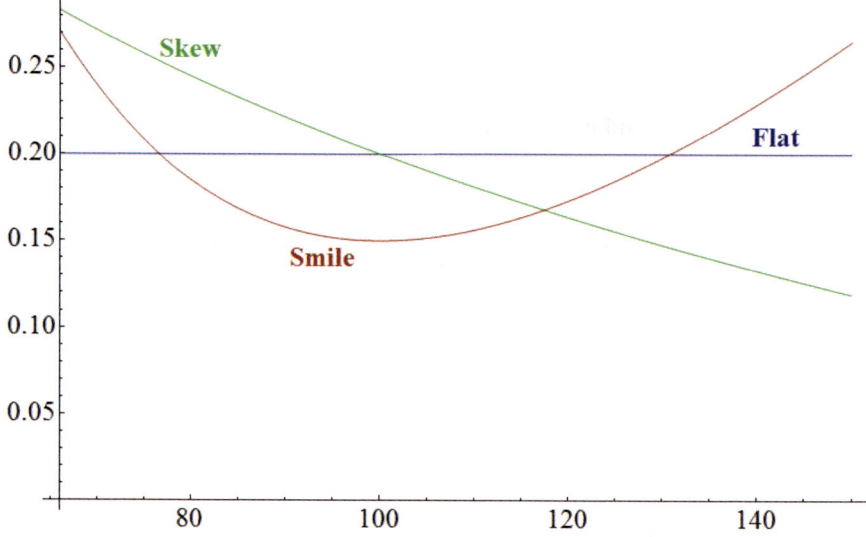

Figure 9.1. Three possible kinds of plots of implied volatility versus strike

The flat line represents the constant volatility assumption of Black-Scholes. Of course, this is not what we see when we look at the implied volatilities of options at different strikes for the same maturity and the same underlying.

In the case of currency options, we often see smiles. It might help to remember it this way by noting that there are traders on both sides of the currency who are buying patriotic calls because they think it will appreciate in value; in other words, if you think of the USD/JPY exchange rate, there are retail American investors buying calls on their own currency versus the yen, and there are retail Japanese investors buying calls on their own currency versus the dollar. Together, they are both buying the wings of the USD/JPY, so we observe a smile. This explanation is not necessarily true, but it is a helpful way to remember that FX options tend to have smiles. Financial hackers love helpful mnemonics. And chocolate.

In the case of index options, where the underlying is eg the S&P 500 index, we observe a skew: the implied volatility of lower-strike options is higher than the implied volatility of higher-strike options.

> Elaine: Don't you find that abnormal?
> Jerry: It is a tad askew.
>
> *Seinfeld* (1994)

In other words, and exaggerating a bit for effect, the implied volatility of a 90-strike option might be 35 while the implied volatility of a 110-strike option might be 25.

Notice the apparent contradiction. We have implied volatilities changing as a function of strike. Those implied vols are calculated by definition using the Black-Scholes model. But in the Black-Scholes model, all volatility is constant. What is going on?

Is it that we are abusing Black-Scholes, forcing it to misprice options and laughing at how poor a job it does? That is probably not the main reason traders continue to look at graphs of Black-Scholes implied volatility day-in and day-out. You rarely see derivatives traders chuckle while looking at such graphs.

On the contrary, they are serious, because there is important information there. Even though the assumptions of Black-Scholes are clearly violated when the implied vols change for different strikes, the implied volatility parameter itself brings with it a host of intuitions.

One could instead simply look at a graph of market prices for options of different strikes. But as we discussed earlier, it is much harder to get intuition about an arbitrary market price than it is to get intuition about an arbitrary implied vol. Recall how much more intuition you have when you are told the implied vol is 5 percent compared to when you are told the option costs 5 cents.

To repeat: the implied volatility is just a non-linear transformation of the market price into a more intuitively understandable and usable number.

Yes, Black-Scholes is wrong. All models are wrong. But it is still incredibly useful. The volatility number is a wonderful, intuitive number. A 20 vol stock feels different than a 30 vol stock or a 50 vol stock. The right way to look at the graph of implied volatility versus strike is through that same lens of feeling.

Consider the case of the skew. An ATM option will have a 20 vol. That means that if the underlying remains near where it is now, its behavior will be like that of a regular 20 vol stock, and we know how that feels.

An option struck at 80 will have a higher vol. That means that as the stock declines, it begins to behave like a more volatile stock would, and we know how that feels.

Finally, an option struck at 120 will have a lower vol. So when this particular stock is being bullish, it will also feel like a less volatile stock.

For an industry that prides itself on math and logic, it is actually these feelings that are the reason we look at graphs of implied volatilities.

> "Mankind are governed more by their feelings than by reason."
>
> *Samuel Adams*

## 9.2 The Ultimate Rogue Trader

Usually the term "rogue trader" is reserved for employees making unauthorized trades, but the meaning is simply a corrupt or dishonest financier. The ultimate rogue trader, the one that would cause the most damage, may be one who is blind to his own corruptness and who is dishonest even with himself.

It is one thing for a firm to be caught unawares by illicit trading activity. It could enforce restrictions to limit the possible size of the damage. But imagine a firm that is taken in by a swindler. It could lose all of its assets willingly and cheerfully. Here comes such a man now.

> "Superstitious man is to the rogue what the slave is to the tyrant."
>
> *Voltaire*

You are sitting in a meeting of the firm's top people. Your boss is there, and your boss's boss. The president. The CEO. The CFO. The general counsel. Are you being fired? No, it looks like you are being promoted!

A man bursts through the room. He is manic, full of energy, jumping around like a crazy person, eyes darting around the room. Everyone stares. You think you recognize him from one of the subsidiary research departments — no, you correct yourself smugly, what will soon be one of *your* subsidiary research departments. You hope no one notices the little smile on your face.

"I've done it!" the man yells. You recall that his nickname around the office is Rock. *Why does everyone on a trading floor have a nickname?* you wonder, but then stop yourself. You daydream too often. You have to cut that out. Especially when there are mad men in the office. You try to stop but you can't keep yourself from wishing that you had a cool nickname too.

"I've got the world's best trade," Rock says. "Pure arbitrage! And best of all, virtually unlimited size!"

Your boss's boss tries to restore calm. "Now is not a good time for this—"

"Nonsense!" says Rock. "It'll only take two minutes and every person in this room will make billions!"

All eyes turn to the CEO. He shrugs and gives a little nod. "Two minutes, go."

*What Rock's got?* you think. *And will I get some credit for it now that I'm about to be promoted?*

"Okay," Rock says and rubs his hands together, something you would have sworn you'd only ever seen done by comic supervillains. "Everybody knows the volatility skew in index options, right?"

Everyone nods. The CEO beckons for him to get on with it.

Rock grabs a green marker from the whiteboard and draws something very similar to the green line of Figure 9.1. "The at-the-money vol is 20," he says, pointing to the middle. "The 80-spot vol is 25 and the 120 is 15." He points these out on the graph too. No objections, though you think he is rounding the numbers a bit.

"What are we talking, three-month S&P?" asks your boss. You understand that he is asking if the skew graph is for three-month maturity options on the S&P 500.

"Sure," Rock shrugs and waves his hand, as if it's not important. *He's not going to win anyone over with that attitude*, you smirk. "Now, the index — the S&P," he nods at your boss, who nods back, "the S&P will have some return from today to tomorrow. Let's say it is up one percent."

He writes "+1%" on the board.

"Then it will have a return from tomorrow till the day after tomorrow. Let's say it's down 2 percent." He writes "-2%" underneath, then three vertical dots. "And so on."

With a furtive glance of your peripheral vision, you get the sense he is losing the room. The faster he is out of here, the faster you will get your new promotion.

"Yeah, and?" you blurt out. *Whoops. That wasn't very professional.*

"And," says Rock, turning to you. "At the end of the three months," nodding again to your boss, "we will be able to calculate the volatility that occurred, right?"

"Right," you say, a little quieter.

"It's just the square root of the average squared deviation from the mean, annualized." He jots down the standard formula. "Suppose it comes out to 20."

"At the end of the time period?" your boss asks.

"Yes, at the end. Now, indulge me for a moment and pretend I can know ahead of time what that number will be." He waves down the resulting eye rolls and protests.

"Do you agree," Rock asks, "that *if* I know the future volatility will be 20, then I can sell the 80-strike puts at 25, and hedge them to 20, and buy the 120-strike calls at 15, and hedge those to 20, and I'd make five vol points of profit on the puts and another five vol points on the call?"

"Yeah," you say, hoping that what you are about to say will crush him, end his intrusion, and get everyone back to your promotion, "but you don't know what the future volatility will be."

"True," he says, pointing at you.

You don't like him pointing at you. And you don't think he's got a good strategy here. Now you hope this interruption won't be counted against you. After all, you haven't even been officially promoted yet. He's not your responsibility yet.

"It might not be 20," he admits. "It might be 25. If it's 25, then I will make nothing on my puts, but I will make ten vol points on my calls."

Aha! Now you've got him. A chance to show everybody how smart you are, how dumb Rock is, and how modest yet efficient you are in meetings. You'll get that promotion for sure.

"Not quite, Rock," you say. "If the true vol is 20 but you hedge to 25, you won't necessarily get ten vol points in total."

"What do you mean?" he asks, bewildered.

"It's because of this hedging to market versus hedging to model thing that I did. I looked into it and ran some simulations. If you hedge to the wrong volatility, you introduce some noise."

"So I might make only eight or nine vol points, or as many as eleven or twelve?"

This was not where you were going with your criticism but now you are trapped. "Uh," you finally manage. "Yeah. Something like that."

"Okay," he says. "So I make ten vol points on average, plus or minus a couple of vol points."

"Right," you say.

"Okay. Still a great trade. But the problem is that I don't know what the future volatility will be. For example, what if it realizes 30 vol?"

He writes this table of numbers on the whiteboard:

|  | Realized: 20 | Realized: 25 | Realized: 30 |
|---|---|---|---|
| Sold puts at 25 vol | +5 | +10 | -5 |
| Bought calls at 15 vol | +5 | 0 | +15 |
| TOTAL | +10 | +10 | +10 |

You follow along and see his point. It doesn't matter what the future volatility is. One option leg will lose on it, but the other will gain. The total profit will always be 10 vol points.

"Of course," Rock says, now nodding towards you, "there is noise in this. If we always hedge to say 20 vol, but the real vol turns out to be 30 or 15 or whatever, we might make eight or nine or twelve vol points. I admit there is some noise. But it's still a great trade. And the key thing is this: I don't have to actually know what the future volatility will be. It can be anything, and I will still make my ten vol points of profit!"

You sneak a peek at the CEO. He seems convinced. He looks at the president. "What do you think?" he asks.

The president shrugs and frowns, somewhat approvingly you think, and turns to your boss's boss, eyebrows raised. Your boss's boss turns to your boss and your boss turns to you. "Your thoughts?"

For the first time in your life, you have no thoughts. You are speechless and thoughtless and just empty all inside.

"Wait a second," the general counsel says, and whispers something in the CEO's ear.

The CEO nods and looks at you. "We have two pieces of good news for you," he says. "When we called you in here, we only had one, but now we have two." He smiles and continues, "First, you are being promoted. You are our new head trader of index options. You will run your own trading desk. Congratulations. And second, this strategy of Rock's is what we want you to implement. You will be working on this 24x7x365. Unless you see any errors in his logic?"

Here you are. The second bit of news is not good, not good at all. Somehow you have ended up reporting to Rocco, in essence if not in form. You have no authority for any new trades or business. All you're going to do is implement his strategy.

You can't come up with a way out later. There would be no way to assemble all of these people back in one room. Especially not if the reason for bringing them all back together is some trivial flaw in Rock's strategy. And if there is a flaw, it is likely to be trivial. It is probably not the case that months of intensive research will uncover a complicated reason why it won't work; it either works or it doesn't work, and if it doesn't work, it would be for a simple reason. And even if you could somehow assemble all these decision makers again in a room in a week or two, and explain to them then the error, they would just ask you why you didn't say so earlier. You'd look bad anyway.

So it is now or never.

Do you see an error in Rock's reasoning? Or will you be spending the rest of your days trying to implement this strategy? What do you do?

> You take a peek outside and observe ferocious looking natives doing a tribal dance around a fire.
>
> You decide to flee. Go to *Page 27*.
>
> You stay: go to *Page 28*.
>
> *Edward Packard*, "Sugarcane Island" (1976)
> (The book that launched the Choose-Your-Own-Adventure series)

## 9.3 Time Freeze

If you ever watched the late 80s sitcom *Out of this World*, then you will remember the little girl who could freeze time by touching her index fingers together. Didn't see it? How about the movie *Casino* where there were lots of freeze frames and voiceover narration? No? What about the end of Rocky III when Rocky Balboa and Apollo Creed begin punching each other and we don't know how the fight ends? Nothing huh. Tough crowd. Okay, just imagine you can freeze time. And you decide to use this superpower to give yourself more time to think.

Let's weigh our options. Is this strategy really pure arbitrage? If so, then perhaps it is your patriotic duty to inform the Federal Reserve and the U.S. government so that they could put it on in even larger size, and maybe balance the budget and pay off the debt. Perhaps you should call an immediate meeting of the International Monetary Fund, the World Bank, and the United Nations. You could be the first global hero!

> "You're in the Naval Reserve, America's seventeenth line of defense, between the Mississippi National Guard, and the League of Women Voters."
>
> *The Simpsons* (1998)

First things first. There is always the obvious objection: if this is such a great idea, why has no one else done it?

> "If he's so smart, how come he's dead?"
> 
> *Homer Simpson*, "The Simpsons" (1999)

There are always only four possible answers to such a question:

(1) Others don't know about it.
(2) Others know about it but simply cannot trade it for some reason.
(3) Someone very big is trading in the other direction.
(4) It's not that great an idea after all.

It's quite unlikely that nobody else knows about this trade. Every single person who has looked at a skew trade could have had the same thought. There is no deep calculation needed to notice that 15 does not equal 25.

It's also unlikely that your company is the only one able to buy and sell options and the underlying. This is the world's most liquid equity index. Everybody can do this trade.

Could it be that someone or some group is throwing billions in the other direction? If you can't even think of what such a shadowy yet powerful cabal might look like, you should probably come to the conclusion, by the cold process of elimination, that you may be missing something in the trade.

Who could it be on the other side? You could run through this argument with Rock, but now that you've frozen time, you can just run it through your own head. One reasonable answer is probably retail investors. They represent enormous piles of money and tend to make similar decisions to each other.

But you still have to come up with a justification for their actions. Here's one attempt: individuals like to buy puts for protection and calls for gambles. For example, if they think Apple will have a meteoric rise, they will buy calls instead of the stock itself, and if they already have a long position in the underlying, they may buy puts to protect themselves on the downside.

In other words, retail investors tend to buy both puts and calls. That would explain why puts have higher implied volatilities on average and calls have... oops. Calls don't have higher implied volatilities on average. This proposed justification is wrong.

> Bart: You're going down, Homer. I'm gonna fool you!
>
> Homer: You talk better than you fool.
>
> Bart: I'll fool you up real nice.
>
> Homer: You couldn't fool your mother on the foolingest day of your life if you had an electrified fooling machine.
>
> *The Simpsons* (1993)

Perhaps there is another group of investors swinging lots of capital behind them. How about institutional investors or funds? They would tend to be buyers of puts for insurance purposes, to protect their downside. And some of them may do what is known as call-overwriting, selling calls to lock in premium at the expense of lower participation in the upside.

At least with this explanation the directions are correct. Extraneous purchases of puts will eventually overflow the available hedging supply from arbitrageurs, raising their implied volatilities, and extraneous sales of calls will eventually oversupply the available hedging demand from arbitrageurs, lowering their implied volatilities. That would indeed create a skew.

It's not clear if there is enough there to create such a large skew, but at least it is something.

Okay, good thing you didn't push through this line of questioning as your only objection to Rock's proposal. He or someone else in the room might have come up with this same scenario, and then you'd be bound to support the project.

Better to object with the strongest argument, one that, if answered, would really sway you to be on board with the trade.

You are running out of time. Even frozen time can thaw and melt. What will you say? What question will you ask, what point will you make, what argument will you advance as to why Rock's proposal to sell downside puts and buy upside calls, and delta hedge both to maturity, will not, and cannot, work?

If you can't think of anything, you're stuck with this job for the foreseeable part of your career. You really need to get out of this situation now, before it consumes your life.

> "Weaseling out of things is important to learn. It's what separates us from the animals! Except the weasels."
>
> *Homer Simpson*, "The Simpsons" (1993)

I have personally asked this puzzle of hundreds of graduate students. Only one got it right. On the flipside, I would bet that just about every experienced derivatives trader *would* get the answer, and it would be blindingly obvious to them.

In fact, it is so blindingly obvious to them, that they probably would never even think to ask it on an interview question. But they might. And you better be prepared with the answer in case they do.

Most importantly, you need to know the answer to this puzzle. And there are only two possibilities: either this is the greatest trade in the world, or you are missing something important and deep.

Hint: this is not the greatest trade in the world.

The best way to show that this is not the greatest trade in the world is to show how some reasonable, plausible model of underlying returns can generate both the implied volatility skew, and a loss to this skew-selling strategy.

The next chapter explains exactly what's going on, but first, we need to discuss some more exotic instruments.

# Chapter 10

# Variance Swaps

Exotic worlds beget exotic swaps. The variance swap is the least exotic. (There is no most exotic.) Understanding how you would have approached the world when variance swaps were first introduced can help you prepare for the new exotic derivatives of tomorrow, where you may well be the very first person to trade them, before valuation software is written, before a model is even hypothesized, let alone tested, before the spreads tighten and the opportunities for first-movers drift away.

## 10.1 Introduction

A variance swap pays off the realized variance of an underlying security or portfolio, relative to a particular strike level. They are a purer way of betting on volatility than options because there is no need to dynamically hedge with the underlying. Whatever the underlying realized volatility will be, that's what you will get.

---

Dwight "The Flight" McGee: Sh#t, that's just too *easy!*

Willy Lewis, correcting him: No, no, no, that sh#t is *too* easy!

Flight: *Too* easy!

Willy: No, no, no. That sh#t is... *too easy!*

Flight: F#@k it. I don't even want to play no more.

Willy: We won't play no more.

*White Men Can't Jump* (1992)

---

Variance swaps are purer, but they are still not pure. We like to think in terms of volatilities, numbers like 20 vol, 30 vol, 50 vol. But variance swaps pay off the square of the volatilities, numbers like .04, .09, .25 that don't convey as much intuition.

Nevertheless, they are more popular than volatility swaps because they are easier to hedge. There exist straightforward valuation methodologies for variance swaps that can in theory replicate the swap payoff with a single, static portfolio of options, and some simple dynamic trading in the underlying. In other words, you can just "set it and forget it" with the options.

You can find those pricing formulas anywhere, and it is a good exercise to implement a variance swap pricer given market prices for options, but our focus here is not on implementing existing models and methodologies. That is something you should do, but you will learn more from trying to do that on your own than you would from yet another derivation of the principles or yet another implementation in some other programming language.

Our focus is not even on deriving new valuation methodologies and elegant formulas. Some financial problems will have elegant solutions and some will not. We should be just as ready to tackle either one.

Instead our focus is on fast, efficient, deep insight.

---

Daniel: What do you expect me to do?

Miyagi: Focus.

Daniel: Oh, great. And what're you gonna do?

Miyagi: Pray.

*Karate Kid 2* (1986)

---

If you think of the timeline involved in new products, those who implement well-established pricing formulas are several years late to the party. Those who completely derive what will eventually become well-established pricing formulas are probably about a year late. The purpose of this book is to make you ready to be the first one to trade, when the new product just comes out, and its mispricing is likely at a maximum, or at the very least at its most volatile. It is in times like those that a prepared, flexible financial hacker and trader can pick attractive spots.

Besides, there will always be new derivatives, new products, and new opportunities. If your tools only apply to particular kinds of opportunities, you are simply less useful than you could be.

## 10.2 Gamma

If we want to make a bet on volatility, why are options not the best way to go? Equivalently, what is the resolution to the puzzle from the previous chapter? We'll now see how everything is related. It all comes down to gamma.

Recall that gamma is the derivative of delta. It is a measure of how sensitive your exposure to the underlying is. Figure 10.1 shows the gamma of a one-year and a one-month option.

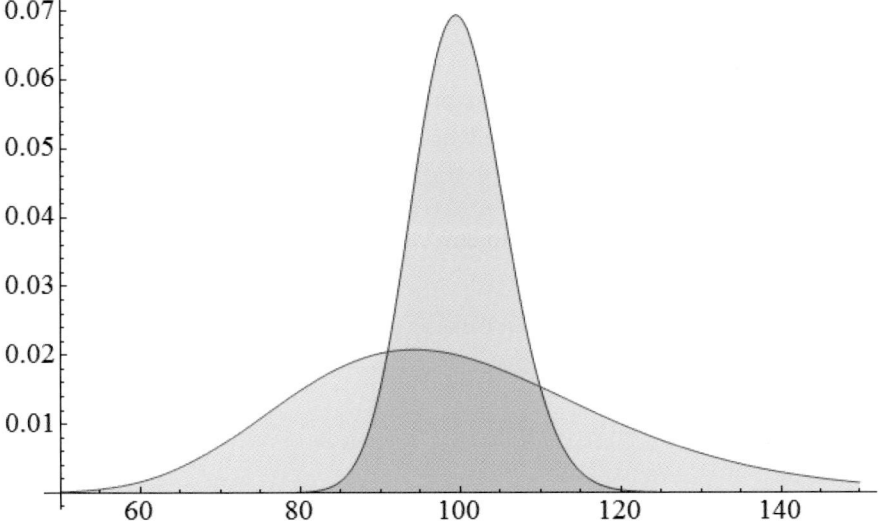

Figure 10.1. The gamma of a one-year (flatter) and a one-month (steeper) option

Notice that the gamma of a call and the gamma of a put are always the same. Why is that?

(a) Because it just works out that way with the particular, specific assumptions of Black-Scholes.
(b) Because forwards have no gamma.

The answer is not (a). The gamma of a call and the gamma of a put will *always* be the same, regardless of the distribution of the underlying. This is because of answer (b), the correct answer. Why does the fact that forwards have no gamma mean that calls and puts have the same gamma?

Because of put-call parity (see Chapter 4). Recall that puts can be created from calls and vice versa with the judicious application of a forward. But forwards have no gamma. They are pure delta-one (or delta-near-one) instruments. So if a call is a put plus some multiple on a forward, then the only gamma an option can have must be the same as for the other option.

> "Dr. David Banner: physician; scientist. Searching for a way to tap into the hidden strengths that all humans have. Then an accidental overdose of gamma radiation alters his body chemistry. And now when David Banner grows angry or outraged, a startling metamorphosis occurs."
>
> *The Incredible Hulk* (1978)

Gamma is what makes options options. Forwards don't have gamma, but neither do deep-in-the-money or deep-out-of-the-money options.

If your call is struck at 100 and the underlying is now at 300, there is virtually no optionality left. Your gamma is zero. It's just a delta-one position.

If your call is struck at 100 and the underlying is at 30, there is again virtually no optionality left. Your gamma is again zero. It is just a delta-zero position.

When you buy and delta-hedge an option, you think that you will make money if the volatility goes up. Say you buy it at 20 vol, but you hope it will realize 30. What if it does realize 30, but only after your option has gone so far deep in the money, or out of the money, that your gamma is zero? Then it is as if you no longer have the option. You only make money on your correct prediction of volatility if you still have gamma exposure at the time the volatility takes place.

Gamma is higher when the underlying is closer to your strike. What about the maturity? From Figure 10.1, we can see that peak gamma is higher when the maturity is lower. So imagine a situation where the maturity is just a few moments away, and the underlying is right near your strike. What does your gamma look like then?

Your call is struck at 100. The underlying is at 101. Expiry is imminent. What do you do?

What is your current position? You are probably short a share of the underlying to hedge your exposure, because your delta is one.

Now let's say the underlying inexplicably jumps down to 99. Are you happy or sad?

Relative to the profit you were expecting to make, you now have an extra two dollars, because you will now choose to not exercise your call, letting it expire worthless, but your short hedge made two dollars. Naturally, you are happy, but being a prudent and conscientious sort, you need to rebalance. After all, your option is about to expire, and if the market rallies immediately after that, you face potentially unlimited losses on your short position.

So you buy back your one share of the underlying. Now you have no position in the underlying and you are long what seems to be a worthless option, with expiration right around the corner.

But wait! The underlying jumps back up to 101, just before expiry. Having lightning quick reflexes, you elect to exercise your call option after all. You just made another dollar out of your seemingly worthless option position.

If the expiry happens right now, you would have made three more dollars than you had just a few seconds ago when the underlying was first at 101. That's the power of gamma near the strike, near maturity.

And imagine that there are still a few clicks on the clock left. Imagine how happy you would be if these see-saw motions in the underlying continue. Each time brings you more money with basically no risk. This is a derivative trader's dream.

But think of the poor sap who sold that option, and is chasing the see-saw motions of the underlying, buying when it goes up, selling when it goes down, all just to hedge his delta. That whiplash is a derivative trader's worst nightmare. There's nothing scarier than being short gamma on a short maturity option near the money.

## 10.3 The Problem with "the Best Trade in the World"

Recall that the alleged "best" trade in the world was to sell the volatility skew of the S&P 500 using index options. Using round numbers, let's say the 80 percent strike puts have an implied vol of 25, the 120 percent strike puts have an implied vol of 15, and the at-the-money vol is 20. The proposal was to sell the downside puts, buy the upside calls, hedge everything to some intermediate vol such as 20, and reap the profits.

---

1. Collect Underpants
2. ?
3. Profit

                        The Gnomes' three-phase business plan, *South Park* (1998)

---

What was the problem with this trade? With our newfound understanding of gamma, the path to the answer becomes clear.

First, consider just the calls. Suppose you buy 120-strike calls at 15 vol and hedge them to the 20 implied vol of 100-strike at-the-money calls. And suppose the realized volatility over the period does end up being 20 vol, just as you predicted. Will you have made 5 vols worth of profit?

Not necessarily, because as we saw, it depends on when (time) and where (price) the volatility primarily took place. If the underlying fell from 100 to 60 and then bounced around down there at 20 vol, your call would have quickly gone from somewhat out-of-the-money to deep out-of-the-money, and your gamma would have gone from small to nothing. Without any gamma, there is no change to your delta, and no way for you to capture the profit from the increased volatility.

Similarly with the puts: you won't necessarily profit from them either, depending on when the volatility takes place.

In fact, you could even end up losing money. How? Suppose the volatility still is 20 on average, but is higher when the underlying is low, and lower when the underlying is high. So let's say the underlying starts at 100 at around 20 instantaneous vol, then dips down to around 80. There, it bounces around a lot more, at say 30 vol. You are short puts there, so short gamma; this excess volatility causes you no end of grief.

*Variance Swaps* 169

Finally, to your huge relief, the underlying trends up, up to where you are long gamma. You rub your hands expecting to make up your earlier hedging losses, but now the underlying is bouncing around a lot *less*. Specifically, it is bouncing around at just 10 vol.

You lost money when you were short gamma because volatility was too high; you lost money when you were long gamma because volatility was too low; and overall you lost money even though the average volatility over the whole period was exactly 20 vol.

## 10.4 Bottom-Up Exotic Simulations

While the previous section completely explains the intuition behind the reason the "best" trade in the world is not necessarily so great, you might want to do some further hacking for two reasons.

First, to convince whoever doesn't buy your verbal argument.

Second, to see if there is a different strategy that might work.

This example also illustrates the broader financial hacking approach of simulating from the bottom-up by fiddling with the mechanics of daily return generation, rather than going from the top-down by fitting a parametric statistical distribution to the observed market values. The latter is the usual approach of financial mathematics and it can result in some beautiful formulas, but the bottom-up approach is more general and provides more intuition.

Can we make some kind of slight change to our random return generator that would result in plausible price paths while also resulting in losses on the skew trade?

One simple change is to replace the assumption of independently random lognormal draws with lognormal draws where the local volatility depends on the level of the underlying.

We can modify the simulation function we've been using since Chapter 6 (page 98) to accommodate any arbitrary local volatility that can be expressed as a function of the most recent underlying price and the current time as measured in years from the starting time.

For example, the linear local volatility function would just be a linearly interpolated number between two known points, each point representing a strike and an instantaneous volatility:

```
Sigma[σ80_ : .3, σ120_ : .1][S_, _] := (S - 80) (σ120 - σ80) / 40 + σ80
```

The Sigma function above does just that, taking as input what we expect the instantaneous local volatility to be when the underlying is at 80, and at 120, respectively. It uses a fun feature of Mathematica that allows you to define functions of functions, so Sigma[.3, .1] returns a function that itself takes two parameters, the current spot price and the current time, and computes the instantaneous local volatility. (It ignores the time altogether, although it could be extended to depend on it too.)

Where do we get the inputs for the local volatility numbers?

(a) Just make them up! Use any numbers you want. That's what financial hacking is all about anyway, right?
(b) Take them to be free parameters and then optimize later to find the best ones.
(c) Use the implied volatilities from the market as a direct proxy for the local volatilities.

If you answered (a), then either you need to reread this book or I need to rewrite it, because that is the very opposite of what financial hacking is all about.

If you answered (b), then you have a mathematical and statistical mind, and are not afraid to make big decisions. You are also either a Libra or a Capricorn. Or, alternatively, we can dispense with the unnecessary horoscope-like analysis of your personality: the reason (b) is not the best answer is because the whole point of financial hacking is how to find quick answers to difficult financial questions.

> "I don't believe in astrology; I'm a Sagittarius and we're skeptical."
> 
> *Arthur C. Clarke*

# Variance Swaps

Optimizing later can be hard. It's certainly not quick; it can't be done in time for a meeting to be held in five minutes. Optimizing later also postpones intuition, and financial hackers want to maximize their intuition per unit time.

If you answered (c), you are still wrong, but it is interesting *why* you are wrong. (The right answer, of course, is none of the above.)

What does it mean if the implied volatility is 20 for an at-the-money option but is 15 for an out-of-the-money option?

It means that the market expects the volatility to fall as the underlying rises. And remember that we just learned that gamma trails off rapidly on options that are deep in- or out-of-the-money or far from maturity. Thus, the only time the implied volatility of that further option will matter is when it ends up near the money at maturity.

If that option does end up near-the-money, then the market is forecasting that the average volatility during its entire tenure would be about 15.

Similarly, if the currently at-the-money option expires near-the-money, then the market is forecasting that the average volatility during its entire tenure would be about 20.

So, the instantaneous volatility today is probably right around 20, because if we stay around here, that's what the market expects us to realize.

But the instantaneous volatility if we end up near the further option's strike is some number $X$ such that the average of 20 and $X$ is 15, because 15 is what the volatility of the entire path ought to be. So obviously $X$ is 10. The instantaneous local volatility when the underlying is at the higher strike price should be 10.

And by the same logic, the instantaneous local volatility when the underlying is at the lower strike price should be 30, so that it averages out to 25 across the entire path.

---

"You know what movies average out to be really good? The first six *Star Trek* movies!"

*Philip J. Fry*, "Futurama" (2002)

172    Financial Hacking

Now we can use a new simulation function that takes a function for its input of volatility and computes it on the fly each day. The problem of course is that such a simulation will be far slower than simply drawing random independent numbers.

But, c'est la vie.

Here is the generalized simulation function:

```
SimulateLV[payoff_, n_ : 10000, μ_ : 0, σFUN_ : Sigma[.3, .1],
  dt_ : 1 / 252, S0_ : 100, maturity_ : 1] :=
 payoff /@
  Monitor[
   Transpose[
    NestList[
     {MONITOR = #[[1]] + 1,
      Function[s,
       s RandomReal[With[{σrdt = σFUN[s, #[[1]] dt] Sqrt@dt},
        LogNormalDistribution[μ dt - σrdt^2 / 2, σrdt]]]] /@ #[[2]]} &,
     {0, ConstantArray[S0, n]}, maturity / dt][[All, 2]]], MONITOR]
```

A word about the Monitor and MONITOR elements there: Monitor[] is a built-in Mathematica function that prints out the value of a variable, which I've called MONITOR in upper case, during the evaluation of the rest of the code. The MONITOR variable is updated to reflect the current day out of 252 days that is currently being evaluated.

The way the code works is to go day-by-day and do all of the simulations, ahem, simultaneously. Each day, for each simulated path, it looks at the preceding spot price and the current time, evaluates the current local volatility, and draws from a lognormal distribution to update the current spot price.

What we want to first do is check the code to ensure it works in the original case of constant local volatility. To do that, we need a function that hedges an option to a given set of prices and at a given fixed hedging vol. This is a generalization of the code in Chapter 6 on page 99:

```
BSHedgeImplVol[prices_, k_ : 100, T_ : 1, σhedge_ : .2, S0_ : 100,
  dt_ : 1 / 252] := BSCallIV[k, T, S0, 0, 0,
  Max[Last[prices] - k, 0] -
   MapIndexed[BSCallDelta[k, T - (First@#2 - 1) dt, #, σhedge, 0, 0] &,
    Most@prices].Differences[prices]]
```

This function calculates the delta-hedged P&L for a given path assuming the deltas are calculated using a constant volatility. This P&L is the replication value of the option along that particular path. We then take that replication value and back out of it the implied volatility at inception. And we do that for every simulated path, so we are left with a distribution of the implied volatility of the option.

The code for the implied volatilities of options are as below:

```
BSOptionIV[payoff_][k_, T_, S_, δ_, r_, Price_, σ1_: .2, σ2_: .3] :=
    Sign[Price] σ /. FindRoot[payoff[k, T, S, σ, δ, r] == Abs@Price,
      {σ, σ1, σ2}, PrecisionGoal → 4];
BSCallIV = BSOptionIV[BSCall];
BSPutIV = BSOptionIV[BSPut];
```

A couple of things to note about the implied volatility code. First, the code for calls and puts are defined in terms of the more general BSOptionIV. Second, unlike traditional implied volatility calculations that assume the price will always be non-negative, this code fits to the absolute value of the given price and then applies the sign of the price to the resulting implied volatility. This way, we can actually get back negative implied volatilities, which can be a useful way of looking at those situations where your hedging actually costs you money.

Figure 10.2 shows that the implied volatility when run on our original assumption of constant 20-vol is indeed tightly centered around 20 vol.

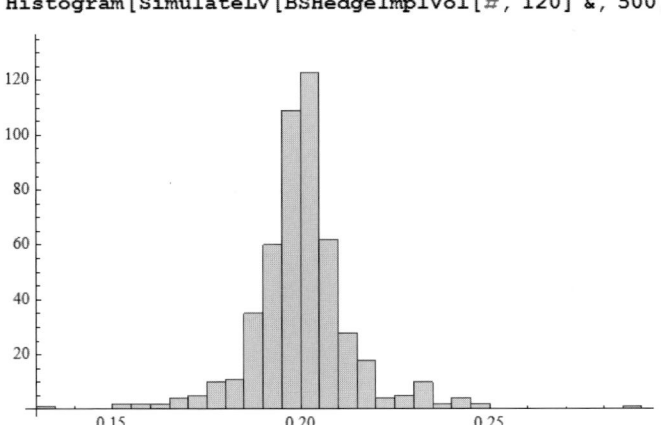

Figure 10.2. Histogram of implied volatility of hedging profit; constant 20 vol

Let's compare this to the situation where we hedge to 20 vol even though the local vol moves from 30 when the spot is 80 to 10 when the spot is 120. Figure 10.3 shows the resulting histogram.

`Histogram[SimulateLV[BSHedgeImplVol[#, 120] &, 500], {.01}]`

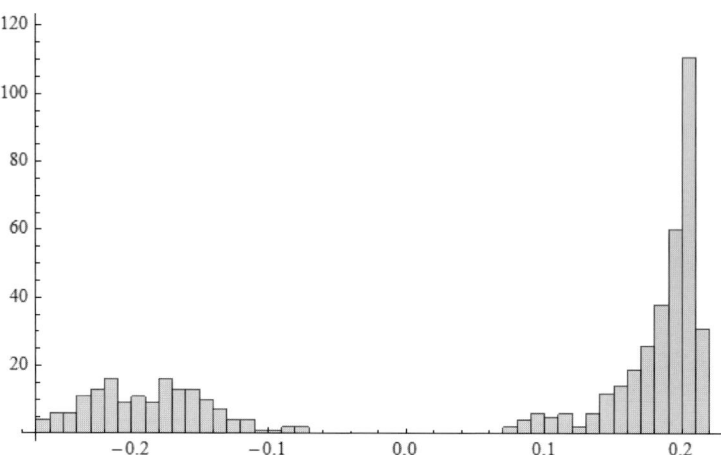

Figure 10.3. Histogram of implied volatility of hedging profit; 30/10 local vol

There are still many times when the implied volatility is around 20 vol, but now there are many times when the implied volatility is actually negative. Of course the implied volatility can never really be negative; this is just a handy way to specify how much losses you could face, in terms of vega.

When is the hedging profit negative? We can rerun the histogram but only focus on paths that either end up above the 120 strike, or have an average above the initial spot, or anything similar. What we find is as expected, that the negative profits come about from paths that tend to spend more time at higher levels of the underlying, when the local volatility is much lower.

> "Up until 35 I had a slightly skewed world view. I honestly believed everybody in the world wanted to make abstract paintings, and people only became lawyers and doctors and brokers and things because they couldn't make abstract paintings."
>
> *Frank Stella*

In short, gamma matters. Selling the skew is a great trade if there is indeed a constant local volatility, regardless of what that local volatility actually is, but when the local volatility moves opposite to the underlying price, selling the skew is a risky trade.

It is also called selling the skew because a distribution that has more volatility to the downside than the upside will appear to have a negative skewness, i.e., fatter left tails than right tails. And that is precisely what we see in the real world.

## 10.5 Constant Gamma and Gamma Buckets

These changing gammas are what drives people to be interested in variance swaps. If you could create a constant-gamma exposure that is the same regardless of the level of the underlying or the time, then you would really be making a bet on volatility, rather than a combined bet on volatility and a hope that it occurs when and where would be beneficial to you.

> Woman: "Why does this dummy have a bucket on its head?"
>
> Kramer: "Because we're blind to their tyranny."
>
> Woman: "Then shouldn't you be wearing the bucket?"
>
> Kramer: "Yeah. Move along, Betty."
>
> *Seinfeld* (1997)

In the meantime, and indeed regardless of whatever derivatives you have on, a common need on the trading floor is to know what exactly your gamma exposure is and will be. What is the best way to make "gamma buckets" for this gamma exposure report?

(a) Split up the options into groups of similar strikes $K$ and maturities $T$, and report the total gamma of options in each bucket of $K$'s and $T$'s.
(b) Calculate the total gamma of all options in the portfolio for different levels of the underlying $S$ and the current time $t$.

> George: "Why is the mailman wearing a bucket?"
>
> Kramer: "Huh? Well, it symbolizes our persecution."
>
> George: "Then... shouldn't you be wearing the bucket?"
>
> *Seinfeld* (1997)

The report in (a) is definitely a bad report. The problem with it is that it aggregates the gamma of subsets of options fulfilling certain criteria on strikes and time to maturity, but what we really want is a scenario analysis of what the total gamma on the portfolio would be for given levels of the underlying and actual time. In terms of the usual variables, we want a report that measures our gamma for various $S$ and $t$, not for various $K$ and $T$.

> Newman: "Kramer, what the hell are you doing?"
>
> Kramer: "I know, I'm gonna switch the bucket to something else."
>
> *Seinfeld* (1997)

The key point to remember is that gamma can come from any option, especially as the underlying moves and time passes. If you restrict your attention only to options with particular criteria, you may miss important gamma exposures.

# Chapter 11

# Esoteric Worlds and Derivatives

Where do you go when you've surpassed exotic? Welcome to the wild uncharted land of esotericism. This chapter presents some final puzzles, examples, and musings to launch you into the rare stratified air above vanilla and beyond exotic where magic reigns and only a few can enter.

## 11.1 Introduction

> "The esoteric teaching was given with the Lyceum in the morning; the exoteric in the evening; the latter related to practice in the art of rhetoric and in disputation, as also to civic business, but the other to the inward and more profound philosophy, to the contemplation of nature and to dialectic proper."
>
> *Thomas Stanley*, "The History of Philosophy" (1701)

The preceding chapters dealt with the nuts-and-bolts of vanilla and exotic derivatives. This chapter focuses on the more profound and esoteric underpinnings of risk and finance itself.

Here we ask questions of a deeper nature.

It is not necessarily the case that the derivatives we will talk about are even more exotic. Indeed they can be vanilla. But the principles we will extract from them are of a more fundamental nature, much like mysticism aims not to dispel other truths but only to help one understand reality on another level.

## 11.2 A Warrant, But Not for Your Arrest

Warrants are just call options issued by the company itself. The primary difference between warrants and listed call options is the effect of *dilution*: the warrants, when exercised, are exchanged into new shares to be issued by the company, rather than previously existing shares to be delivered by the counterparty.

There are two interesting warrant puzzles, one easy and one devious.

The easy one is this: compare two different companies, A and B, that until now have been identical in all respects. Now, company A issues an at-the-money warrant maturing in five years. It issues it for a fair price so that its underlying equity price is unaffected. (If it had issued it below fair value, its equity price would have dropped, just as it would with any poor investment decision. Let's assume the price was fair.)

You can buy one five-year at-the-money warrant from company A for $1. How much would a five-year at-the-money vanilla call option on company B cost in the market place?

(a) More than $1.
(b) Less than $1.
(c) Equal to $1.

You might think that they are both ultimately options, so from the perspective of a buyer, answer (c) would be correct. You'd be wrong.

Think of what happens at maturity. Suppose both companies have soared over the preceding five years. Warrant holders and option holders all want to exercise. Let's say both originally had 10 shares outstanding.

The option holder of company B would receive ten percent of the value of the company once he chooses to exercise. But the warrant holder of company A would receive one new share out of the now total eleven shares, so he would have about nine percent of the company.

---

Simon: Meet Maggie Simpson, IQ 167.

Lisa: But, but my IQ is only 159! Maggie's more intelligent than me?

Simon: That's right, because 167 is a bigger number than 159. Do you see how that works?

Lisa: [annoyed] Yes, thank you.

*The Simpsons* (2004)

Nine is a smaller percentage than ten, and since we've assumed the two firms have grown identically from fundamental assets, the warrant holder of company A will have a smaller amount of wealth than the option holder of company B.

That was the easy puzzle. Now it's time for the devious one. It is particularly devious because you don't know if I am saying it is devious for reasons of counter-intuitiveness or counter-counter-intuitiveness, i.e., one of those times when your first hunch turns out to be right even though it feels wrong.

Consider now just company A, same as above, who issues five-year at-the-money warrants. Company A also has a vibrant listed options market. The warrant again costs $1. How much would the five-year at-the-money listed call option cost?

(a) More than $1.
(b) Less than $1.
(c) Equal to $1.
(d) Depends on the number of shares outstanding.

The knee-jerk reaction is to think that again the answer is (a), because of dilution making the warrant worth less. But the answer is (c).

True, dilution affects the value of the warrant such that it costs less than an equivalent option on a different company that had never issued a warrant. But dilution affects the value of the listed option on the same firm in exactly the same way as it affects the warrant!

We can even prove it by arbitrage.

Let's say the warrant costs less than the option. Then we buy the warrant and sell the call and pocket a small difference in premium. Now, whenever the option holder informs us they want to exercise, we will exercise the warrant. The option holder was expecting existing shares, not new shares, but once the new shares are issued, they are all fungible, meaning exchangeable with each other. And if the option holder allows the options to expire worthless, we too can let the warrant expire worthless.

In other words, it is a perfect hedge. And the initial excess premium we pocketed was pure arbitrage.

## 11.3 The Curious Case of Convertible Bonds

Convertible bonds can seem to be relatively simple instruments. While perhaps technically they are exotic because of the interplay between debt, credit, equity, and volatility, they are ultimately little more than gussied-up vanilla calls.

A convertible bond is a fixed income instrument that pays out a regular coupon and a final payment like a regular bond but which can be instead exchanged into a number of shares of the company in certain circumstances at the option of the holder.

More complicated hair in the CB world can include mandatory conversion in certain circumstances, contingent conversion, and more. It can be very difficult to build a completely general convertible bond pricer because of all of these various features; new features routinely come out as well.

But what makes CB's an interesting example for this deeper chapter on esoteric finance is not the fact that it can be more complicated, but the impact it can have on the underlying.

> "The whole secret of the teacher's force lies in the conviction that men are convertible. And they are. They want awakening."
>
> *Ralph Waldo Emerson*

Suppose a company issues a very large CB and let's say its embedded option gives bondholders the right to convert at an effective strike of 200 in ten years.

Before the bond issue, regular options at that strike and that maturity traded at a 20 implied vol.

What should happen to the implied vol after the massive new CB issue?

(a) It should remain about the same.
(b) It should go up a little.
(c) It should go down a little.

The answer isn't quite none of the above this time; it's any of the above, depending on a few things. The key insight though is this: the company doesn't hedge its issuance. No company issues CBs and starts delta hedging its daily exposure by buying back some shares.

But the CB buyers, such as hedge funds, proprietary trading desks, and the like, typically *do* hedge. And that trading activity might have an effect on the underlying. What does the size of the effect depend on?

Recall that gamma is highest near maturity, near the money. If the stock really is around 200 in ten years, then every time the stock randomly ticks up, a flurry of sales orders from CB hedgers will trample it back down, and when the stock randomly ticks down, a bevy of buys will lift it back up. The effect could be smaller, but still noticeable, even farther away from the strike or earlier in time.

What will the impact depend on?

(a) The average daily trading volume of the stock.
(b) The amount of the convertible bond originally issued.
(c) The percentage of the bond still outstanding.
(d) The gamma at the particular stock level and time.
(e) The market impact of large orders.
(f) The expected daily volatility if there were no hedgers.

The answer is all of the above, except not so much on (f). If there is a lot of trading volume, if the amount of the CB issued or still outstanding is small, if the underlying liquidity is so large even with small volume that large orders can be easily handled by the market, or if the gamma itself is small, then the impact could be quite negligible.

The "natural" daily volatility, or what would have happened in the absence of hedgers, is not that important because ultimately the impact of the hedgers will be proportional to the natural volatility. Taking into account all of the other factors, the impact might be to squeeze volatility by half, for example. This squeezing is virtually independent of the original level of the volatility; it is merely a proportionate reduction. So it is important, but not as much, because it does not affect the proportion by which the impact reduces the volatility.

This is the phenomenon known as squeezing to the strike, when holders of derivatives with long gamma tend to hedge while the sellers of those derivatives with short gamma tend not to hedge. If both sides hedged, then their trading would offset each other and we would experience the natural volatility.

The opposite phenomenon exists too. In the case of mandatory conversions, bondholders are effectively short a put, because they may receive stock shares against their will instead of bond payments. Now the bondholders are short gamma while the company, which does not hedge, is long gamma. This can actually exacerbate volatility as hedgers chase upticks up and downticks down.

> "As love without esteem is capricious and volatile; esteem without love is languid and cold."
>
> *Jonathan Swift*

## 11.4 The Bad Path Puzzle

Look back at the negative hedging P&L of Figure 10.3 resulting from hedging to a fixed 20 vol when the local vol varies from 30 to 10. Those are symptomatic of a more general phenomenon. Even the histogram in Figure 10.2, hedging to 20 vol when the underlying is 20 vol, can result in hedging losses with enough simulations. To exaggerate the effect, hedging to a 20 vol when the underlying is 15 vol can result in frequent hedging losses.

All of these seemingly anomalous negative results can be simplified to the following bad path puzzle.

The underlying is at 100. You buy an out-of-the-money 120-strike call expiring in a few days. It cost you some amount of money.

Being a conscientious trader, you immediately hedge your delta. Your delta is not 50 or probably even 40 since you are out-of-the-money, but it is something. So you sell some shares at 100.

The next day, the stock goes up, to say 105. Your delta increases so you need to hedge some more. You sell some shares at 105.

Say this happens a few more days.

On the last day, the day of expiry, the stock ends at 120. You are right at the money; a little more and you would have had some intrinsic value. Your option expires worthless, and you buy back your shorts to zero out your positions. What is your P&L?

You paid something for an option that expired worthless; that's a loss. You sold shares at 100, at 105, and so on, and bought them back at 120; each of those was a loss. You have two losses and no gains and no other securities or instruments.

How could it be that you end with a negative P&L? You did everything by the book, Black-Scholes style. We've assumed away frictions and transactions costs and interest rates and dividends.

Is this a bug in Black-Scholes? Have all our previous tinkerings been for naught? What can explain this puzzle?

The problem is the lack of continuous hedging. The probability of three consecutive up ticks is about $1/2^3 = 1/8$; for four it is $1/16$; for an infinite number of ticks it is zero. It simply can't happen. In continuous time, there would be enough up-and-down movements to make delta-hedging worthwhile.

In real discrete life, it does happen, and you have to watch out for it.

## 11.5 The Road Ahead

I hope you never read this book again.

It is not intended as a reference. Finance is not about looking up the formula and plugging in numbers; at least, cutting-edge finance isn't. It is about logic and quick thinking and intuition. It is about what used to be called back-of-the-envelope calculations, except no one uses envelopes anymore.

New derivatives will come and go. New opportunities. If you are able to assess and exploit them quickly, I hope you will find a career in finance and risk that can be highly rewarding and personally enjoyable.

Have fun.

---

"To infinity... and beyond!"

*Buzz Lightyear*, "Toy Story" (1995)